# Cruising

## THE BOATS AND
## THE PLACES

# BILL ROBINSON

# Cruising

## THE BOATS AND
## THE PLACES

W · W · NORTON & COMPANY
NEW YORK  LONDON

Designed by Earl Tidwell

Library of Congress Cataloging in Publication Data

Robinson, William Wheeler, 1918–
    Cruising, the boats and the places.

    1. Yachts and yachting. I. Title
GV813.R58     1981     797.1     80–16229
ISBN 0–393–03258–2

W. W. Norton & Company, Inc. 500 Fifth Avenue, New York, N.Y. 10110
W. W. Norton & Company Ltd. 25 New Street Square, London EC4A 3NT

1 2 3 4 5 6 7 8 9 0

Dedicated to

ROSEMARY CURLEY,

my assistant of many years, for her unfailing
cheerfulness in carrying out all sorts of tasks,
including a great deal of help with this book.

# Contents

~~~~~~~~~~~~~~~~~~~~~~~~~~~~~~~~~~~~~~

Contents

PART III: *Where to Cruise*

## Contents

# Introduction

One trick of mine to while away the long, dark hours of trying to stay awake at the wheel on a night watch is to make up lists. Countries visited; what states I've slept in; places I've played squash—any inane category capable of producing a list is enough to pass a good part of a watch, and one that I happened to hit on set me to thinking. I tried to remember, going back to the first one in 1932, all the cruises I've made in other people's boats. By the time I got to 1978, I'd hit sixty, and then I started trying to separate in my mind all the cruises my wife, Jane, and I have taken in the three sloops we've owned, and I got up past fifty before I was relieved of the watch and hit the sack. Why not, came the thought, collect this data into a book, along with information on the areas we've cruised? Cruising auxiliaries and their specifications, characteristics, special features, rigs, layouts, sailing qualities, and general suitability are of endless fascination to cruising addicts. Everyone is forever seeking the perfect boat, always working through compromises of some sort, and it's amazing how many variations on a basic function there can be. That this creates lively interest is graphically demonstrated at the in-water boat shows, where visitors spend hours crawling from boat to boat, often waiting in line for a chance to study the features on the latest offering from a designer or manufacturer.

Naturally I don't have vital statistics on all the sixty or so OPBs (Other People's Boats) I've cruised in, but quite a few of the newer ones are still fresh in mind and have information available (starting with the smallest and working up the size scale). As for the cruising areas, they do remain clearly in memory. I don't propose a full cruising guide on each one of them, telling you where to buy bread and what tree to take a range on. There are annually issued guides for most cruising grounds (referred to when applicable in the chapters to come), and they do a fine job. They do need an annual update, though, as facilities change and key people are in a constant turnover. Often, even in the annually amended guides, someone touted as the key person to see in a given port will have already eloped with the innkeeper's wife, hit the bottle, or gone cruising himself by the time the information is in print. So the intention here is merely to give a general picture of what each cruising area is like: what to expect in the way of wind, weather, harbors, preferred season, and general atmosphere—items that don't change quite as rapidly as the condition of facilities and the whims of personalities.

As for the boats, this is naturally not an all-inclusive catalog, as each boat is written up from personal experience, and even an editor on a yachting magazine can't get around to all the boats of a given type. I think they do give a well-rounded picture of what has been available in cruising auxiliaries in recent years, however, and the various solutions to inevitable compromises that they represent. The many ways to balance size, price, accommodations, sailing ability, looks, and rig are all included. As to what makes the ideal cruising auxiliary, one man's meat is another man's Pearson, and I'll leave your own answer up to you. Everyone has a different one. The way I arrived at mine will be covered later.

# PART I

*Thinking, Buying, and Bareboating*

# Thoughts on Cruising

Why do people cruise in sailboats?

Certainly not as an efficient means of transportation, since sailboats lost top ranking in that category over a hundred years ago. Still, today there are probably at least as many people cruising for pleasure in sailboats as there were professional American seamen in the heyday of commercial sail. Sailboats have made the transition from the hard world of commerce to the relaxed one of pleasure boating, refusing to die out like the horsecar when its earning days came to an end, and a whole new psychology, a new attitude toward being afloat under sail has developed. Cruising for pleasure is a relatively new concept, dating only to the late nineteenth century for all but a few special cases, and it really was not until the post–World War II era that any significant number of people took it up. In the 1930s, Cuttyhunk was a hideaway known only to a select few, a boat could go for days along the Maine coast without encountering another yacht or lose itself in solitude throughout the Chesapeake's hundreds of byways, and as for the Bahamas and Virgin Islands, only the most adventurous long voyagers had tasted their delights.

The ingredients have always been there for a most relaxing, rewarding way of getting away from one's usual surroundings into a whole new world, one confined to the immediate horizon, the nearest landfall, and the tidy dimensions of a sailboat. To spend a day in competition with nature—sometimes more a mild embrace than a contest, sometimes a severe challenge of muscles, stamina, and willpower—and then achieve, at the end of it, the peace and security of a new harbor, has a strong, continuous, and repetitive appeal. More and more sailors have succumbed to the appeal in all its variations, and variations there are, ad infinitum as an integral part of the appeal.

A port that has few pretensions to glamor when approached by

*Modern marinas have developed a special lifestyle. Newport Harbor, California.*

land transportation takes on new charm when it is reached at the end of a day's sail. There are new dimensions to it and new vistas, and the sense of having accomplished something in getting there adds to the reward. There are also, of course, ports that cannot be reached by anything but an approach by water, and these are even more special in their rewards to the cruising sailor.

Cruising has many definitions to those who call themselves cruising people. There are the marina huggers, who can never get too far away because the poodle has to be walked twice a day (although these are more often in powerboats), there are the ten-to-three passagers with perhaps a stop for lunch, the sightseers who only cruise as a means of seeing new places, and their opposites, the hairy-chesters who like nothing better than a hard, spray-flinging thrash from dawn to dusk. For them, the actual sailing, the rush of the hull through the water, the trim of the sails, and the look and feel of the seas as they sweep by is all. The ports and shore excursions don't matter. The ultimate in this breed is the offshore passagemaker whose only dream of cruising is to head for Hawaii, Tahiti, or the Azores, locked in a private world of sea, sky, and small boat for day after day. Among these, the sole voyager is an even more specialized cruising person, and fairly often the separation from all else in the world is more a private psychological escape syndrome than a pure love of sailing.

In more than one hundred cruises, I have seen all of it but the long solo passage offshore. I am not interested in that sort of thing for myself, and I find that very few people actually are, although those who do it make such an impression that they perhaps seem like a larger group than they are. All I know is that I am not that type of loner. I like to swim, but I am never going to swim the English Channel or the Straits of Florida, and long solo voyaging is to me a nautical equivalent of that sort of thing.

Over the years, I have developed some thoughts and opinions on what works and what doesn't work in the kind of cruising that gives the most pleasure to the greatest number of people—coastal cruising, harbor-to-harbor each day. This can be in one's own boat or in one of the continuously increasing number of bareboats that are now available in so many areas. The makeup of the crew brings variations, of course. If it is a family with young children, one couple, several couples, or a stag group of experienced sailors, the routines and governing considerations will be very different.

There is one cardinal rule that applies to all, however: don't try to do too much.

"Too much" depends on variations in crew as mentioned above, but an unfortunate number of cruises are ruined each year because of too ambitious an itinerary. In port-to-port cruising, I like to use thirty miles as a rule of thumb for a successful day. I have done as much as sixty miles in a 24-footer when the wind was right and daylight hours were long, and making a forty- to fifty-mile day in larger boats has been an easy, delightful experience, again because of conditions. If you are on a delivery schedule or making time down the Intracoastal Waterway, that is another matter. I am talking here of an easy-going vacation cruise within a given area. A thirty-mile (or less) day usually means a relaxed start after a comfortable breakfast and cleanup, and if everyone has also had time to go to the head, find sunglasses, knitting, or novel, and put on sunburn cream, it will be a happier crew. Many a time Jane has had to make breakfast underway or at least do the dishes after we have started, but in general the slow-starting days are the nicer ones.

Even with a relaxed start, a thirty-mile day usually allows arrival at a decent afternoon hour (decent being before 1700, more or less). In some areas this is necessary simply for finding a berth or anchorage in some of the more popular harbors, and the situation has gotten tough enough in many busy spots to require an advance reservation at marina or club mooring.

In compact areas with a wide choice of harbors, like the Virgin Islands, the Maine coast, or the Chesapeake, a swim and lunch stop is a pleasant amenity (don't bother with the swim in Maine unless you belong to your local Polar Bear Club). In planning a cruise itinerary, it is a good idea to provide for a layday of some sort, both to allow for bad weather that might upset a tight schedule and to vary the routine with some sightseeing ashore, a snorkel or scuba expedition, or perhaps some fishing. This is especially important with youngsters along.

Since weather is the key to pleasant cruising, it is important to know as much about it as possible at all times and to use it in planning a given day. Off the continental U.S. the continuous NOA weather broadcasts, usually on 162.55 mHz, are the best you can do, although they are far from infallible. We have found the Florida ones particularly helpful in keeping track of approaching cold fronts, but the broadcasts in the Hatteras area, for example, have had a low percentage of accuracy when we followed them because of the unpredictability of the weather there, where many elements clash and combine erratically. In boating areas there is at least one commercial station that provides marine weather, sometimes with helpful interpretation by a commercial (as opposed to governmental) meteorologist. In any event, use all the information you can get, and try to become familiar with local danger signs. On our home river, thunderstorms always come from the same direction, right over a church steeple on an inland hill. When the steeple stands white against developing black clouds, it is time to take shelter. In the Bahamas, the cycle of wind directions can tell you a lot, and when the wind goes around to south or southwest and blows fresh,

*A cruising harbor in the British Virgins—Cooper Island.*

you know that a cold front is on the way fairly soon, with a switch to strong northerlies. Every area has its idiosyncracies that can be learned to advantage.

Charts and guidebooks, needless to say, are mandatory, and most cruising areas now have good annually issued guides, like the *Waterway Guides* on the East Coast, the *Yachtsman's Guides* in the Bahamas and West Indies, and the *Sea Almanacs* on the Pacific Coast. There are many hardcover guides that are generally helpful, although much of the specific information can become quickly outdated. The *Stone and Hart Cruising Guide to the West Indies* is a classic reference of general conditions and basic advice, but should be supplemented with annuals as well. I have become so accustomed to using guides and expecting them that I feel quite cheated in an area that does not have one.

Guides are a great help in choosing nightly anchorages, and from what I have seen of cruising boats in all parts of the world, anchoring is one of the biggest headaches, especially for part-time cruising people

21

who perhaps charter once a year. It is always amazing, and sometimes amusing, to watch a boat come into a crowded anchorage under a full head of steam and suddenly come to a stop with no regard for wind or current direction. Then the anchor is shot-putted into space in a flying tangle of line and chains, or just let go in a headlong crash, and without even checking whether it is holding or whether the scope will bring the boat up against a neighbor in a wind shift, the crew settles down to cockpit revelry. This sort of thing usually ends in an 0300 crisis of bouncing off a nearby boat, or of dragging off into the night.

Just as ineffectual is the nervous-nelly type who spends hours backing and filling around the anchor, usually with acrimonious communication between husband on bow and wife at the controls, and the husband giving his most critical commands facing forward so they can't be heard at the wheel. I am guilty of this latter sin on occasion, easy to do when the anchor is engaging all your efforts, and we have therefore developed simple hand signals for forward, neutral, reverse, and rudder directions. They do save a lot of shouting.

There is no magic to proper anchoring procedure. It is simply a case of common sense in choosing a spot that will clear all neighboring boats in any wind or current direction, remembering that where the anchor is dropped, not where the boat ends up, is the key spot. Once this is selected and the depth checked, the boat should be headed into the wind or current, whichever is stronger, and put in reverse slowly (or allowed to drop back in irons if you are a purist anchoring under sail) until you have almost the desired scope out. Scope depends on type of anchor, amount of chain, strength of wind, and type of bottom, but somewhere between a three to one and five to one scope to depth should usually be it. Snub the anchor and see if it is holding. The quickest way to check this is to watch the stern. If it starts to swing back and forth instead of sagging in one direction, your anchor has taken hold. A foot or hand on the rode will tell if it is in tension and holding.

Once this is done, let more rode out to the desired scope and make fast. One short burst in reverse then helps to set the anchor further (or will break it out if it is not in properly). Once it is set, pick a visual bearing on landmarks on shore that can be checked later on.

*The morning after some careless anchoring the night before.*

The anchor itself is a subject open to much discussion, and the type of anchor used depends on personal choice, type of boat, and type of bottom. In cruising in all parts of the world, I have ended up liking the CQR or plow anchor as the best all-around compromise, and we have generally had good luck with it in our own boats and in chartered ones. It has no bad weaknesses and it is generally more adaptable to a variety of bottom conditions than others we have used. I particularly like the way it can be stowed in a bow chock, which we have had on our last two boats, as this saves a great amount of fuss, muss, and back strain in getting it aboard, and leaves it in position for quick use if there is that need. If you really worry about your back, an anchor windlass might be a good investment.

The only failure we have had with a plow was on hard grass in Governor's Harbour, Eleuthera. On a night of very little breeze, we persisted in dragging slowly across the harbor, perhaps one hundred feet an hour, as the anchor could not be made to dig in. Probably the only solution here would be to dive down and set the anchor manually, which I was not about to do after dark (swimming after dark where sharks can be found is asking for trouble). I don't think that any other type of anchor would have done any better, and one thing about the plow—it drags slowly, which sometimes happens in soft mud or loose sand, rather than pulling out all of a sudden and casting you adrift. If bearings are checked occasionally when there is some doubt, you should be on top of the situation.

The plow also snags less and can usually be freed from a jam in coral or rock by putting a strain on it at short stay in several different directions.

For one-directional pull once properly set there is no beating the Danforth anchor and the many types that now use variations on the same principle. They give the best weight-to-holding-power performance, and an amazingly small anchor will hold a big boat if given enough scope so that the pull is as horizontal as possible, with little vertical force. This makes for an excellent lunch hook and for real security when a strong blow remains in the same direction. The weakness here is that a quick shift of direction can pull the anchor loose suddenly and it might not reset itself at the new angle. Also, there is vulnerability to snags like a beer can or clam shell caught between the flukes (or something impaled on the point of one). Then it becomes inoperative.

The old-fashioned navy anchor, with the stock at right angles to the flukes, is effective (but not in proportion to its weight), is a knuckle buster to handle and stow, and can become fouled if the boat circles around it during wind or current changes, as the rode can wind around the stock and break the anchor loose with no chance of resetting. Other variations of a right-angled stock have the same weakness, and stockless anchors, like the kind you see hanging from the hawse hole of big ships, must have tremendous weight to be effective.

An important basic adjunct to the anchor is a shot of chain attached to it. This is vital for keeping the angle of pull as horizontal as possible, and very often, in light weather with no chop or surge to worry about a boat will be riding to the weight of the chain lying on the bottom, with almost no strain on the anchor. When the tension is greater in strong breezes, the chain still tends to keep the angle of pull low, and it is an important factor in avoiding chafe in coral areas, or where there are sharp rocks that might fray rope. In Australia, cruising near the Barrier Reef in coral-strewn harbors, we found that the bareboat charter yachts had all chain for their anchor rodes—hard on the back when weighing, but easier on the mind otherwise.

Being basically lazy (and weak in the back, too), I like to find a mooring whenever possible instead of anchoring, but a strange mooring should never be used without finding out what it consists of. You should always have permission by prearrangement or by checking with a launch man or the harbor master before picking up a mooring.

More and more we have become a marina society, and I for one certainly sleep better when snug in a slip. What you gain in the amenities of shore power, showers, laundry, shopping, and perhaps a restaurant in marina living has to be balanced against the fee and loss of privacy. Much depends on the area and the type of cruise, but an occasional marina stop certainly makes life easier. In some areas, such as Southern California, and in many European ports, there is no choice but to go to a marina.

Eating is important whenever you are on land or sea, and providing for it on a boat is an extra challenge requiring special planning. This is such a personal matter that it is impossible to give even general advice, and whole books have been written on cruising cookery. Again the dictum of not doing too much generally applies, and I personally prefer simplicity aboard with meals that are easily prepared and cleaned up after, but there are those who take special delight in all sorts of gourmet treats as part of a cruise, and more power to them if they can handle it and find it fun.

The same rule of "Don't try to do too much" should also be applied to the galley department, especially, as is so often the case, if the cruise is supposed to be a vacation. Mom does not consider it one if she is tied to the galley a good part of the day. To my mind, eating dinner ashore when the opportunity and the budget allow is an important ingredient in successful cruising, especially in areas where there are good local specialties like fish and lobster in New England, oysters and crabs in the Chesapeake, and Dungeness crabs in the Pacific Northwest. In foreign areas it can be a vital part of the adventure to eat

*An inflatable carried on deck is a good solution to the dinghy problem.*

ashore. We got a great kick out of trying our luck in little country inns of the Fyn Archipelago in Denmark; Corsica and Sardinia had interesting places to eat; and the Aegean is always an adventure in that department.

In most cruising, a dinghy is an absolute must. Unless you are in an area where all your stops are in marinas, you can't get along without one. If your boat is under 30 feet, stowing a dinghy on board can be a real problem, and I never feel completely easy when towing one, although it is absolutely standard procedure in the southern bareboat fleets. There, the operators have developed dinghies that are tough and tow well and easily, even in rough going, and they are almost never lifted aboard. The outboard remains on the transom, tipped up when not in use. These boats are either fiberglass or aluminum, and relatively maintenance free, and it is remarkable what a dinghy with good sheer, flared bow, and modified-V bottom with minimum deadrise can take in the way of sea conditions. Usually, there is a spot in the wake pattern of the towing boat that determines the best length of the dinghy painter, very often the point where the second set of waves from the wake vees out from the center of it.

Despite their adaptability to towing, dinghies must be brought aboard for open-water passages. This is always a problem on the relatively cluttered deck of a cruising auxiliary, where they often impede ease of moving around the deck, are a nuisance most of the time, and can be a danger in an emergency. But there is usually some solution by placing the dinghy across the foredeck or the transom, or on the cabin trunk. Carrying one on davits over the stern has some advantages, but this adds weight and expensive equipment in an awkward place, hurts visibility in many cases, and can be a hazard if there is a danger of being pooped in a following sea. And, of course, part of the drill of maneuvering for anchoring or entering marinas should be a shortening of the dinghy painter to keep it from fouling the propeller. There are no statistics on how often this happens, but I'll bet they would be impressive if compiled.

Considering everything, my personal preference is for an inflatable. These have become thoroughly reliable in construction and will take an amazing beating. If not needed, they can be easily stowed when deflated, such as on an Intracoastal Waterway trip when you do not plan to anchor out, and they are easily handled on and off the boat by one person, a real problem with rigid dinghies. Our present boat has a raised-deck cabin with plenty of room for the dinghy, so that is no problem. Be sure to analyze stowing possibilities on your own deck before choosing a dinghy.

Although an outboard is a great convenience on the dinghy, and almost a must in some areas, we have gotten along without one without too much of a problem, avoiding two nuisances—maintenance of the motor and stowage of gasoline on board (I feel much easier with no gasoline at all aboard the boat).

All these are general thoughts on my own preferences based on my own experiences, and I am always a bit taken aback by the number of people who disagree with what I think are eminently sensible ideas. Since everything to do with a boat is a compromise of some sort, it is part of the fascination of dealing with boats to arrive at your own best compromises. How they apply to choosing a boat comes next.

# Choosing a Boat

It's always interesting to arrive at a solution to your own problems, perfectly convinced that your thinking and reasoning are correct, only to find that someone else has supposedly put equally as much thought into similar problems and come up with a very different answer. This couldn't be more evident than in the two models of our latest acquisition, a CSY 37 cutter (named *Brunelle*). This model is offered in two layouts. One provides a tricabin arrangement, with two private staterooms, each with its own head, and a main cabin with a dining area and a settee that makes up into upper and lower berths if needed (see page 111). Naturally, in 37 feet, even with a raised-deck configuration and plenty of beam (12 feet), this layout means that the boat is rather cut up down below and no one cabin looks like a grand ballroom. It was designed for use in the Caribbean sailing yacht's bareboat fleets in southern waters, where many of these boats go.

The alternative layout calls for a single stateroom with double berth forward to port, and an open main cabin with a big dining area and an open galley to port at the after end. A settee can be converted to upper and lower in the main cabin, but this is essentially a one-couple boat, arranged for marina living. This is very evident in the location of the only head. It is right up in the forepeak (in the area that originally gave the head its nautical name), which makes for a roomy set-up in port, but I hate to imagine what using this facility in a strong head sea offshore would be like. A seatbelt would be required equipment for anyone trying to sit there with the boat plunging and rearing. Untenable is the word, I believe.

And yet the builder has had more orders for this layout than for the tricabin one. Whether people have analyzed what they really want and need or have just succumbed to the admittedly impressive openness of the main cabin is a question I can't answer. Certainly anyone

28

who has ever made an offshore passage would think twice before choosing this layout, attractive as it is in a boat-show setting, and any overnight guests would feel like poor cousins in it. It certainly wouldn't work for chartering.

As for our own thinking, we set the parameters of our own requirements and then looked for a boat that fit them, and this is the way it went. Ours called for a boat between 35 and 40 feet, so that Jane and I could handle her by ourselves in normal port-to-port cruising. (Even if I could afford one, I don't want a boat over 40 feet. Then the gear gets bigger, the sails are harder to handle, and getting under way, anchoring, maneuvering around slips, and maintenance all become more of a chore. If we were a bit younger and more gazelle-like we might not feel this way, but we've found this size range ideal for us.) And the original price, and the operating and maintenance costs, go up more in geometric than in arithmetic progression above the 40-foot barrier.

In this size range we wanted a boat that would provide real comfort and privacy for two couples. We cruise by ourselves a lot, but we like to entertain family and friends, and we like more hands aboard for offshore passaging, even if only for an overnight trip. To do this right calls for two private cabins and two heads. Until you have cruised with these amenities you don't realize what a difference they make in comfort and in the relaxed relationship between couples. This is especially true for women guests who may not be experienced at cruising and may feel uneasy and embarrassed at the usual intimacy and lack of privacy in a single-head layout.

This may seem unnecessarily fussy, but it really is important. If your guests are edgy and ill at ease, there is a completely different atmosphere aboard. The ideal plan for privacy is a center cockpit layout with separate after cabin. We had this in our previous boat, *Tanagra*, a Morgan Out Island 36 (see p. 101), and we were quite happy with it. The cabin was very comfortable and we could have been at opposite ends of the *QE2* as far as privacy was concerned. Some knowledgeable sailors, especially the naval architect Frank MacLear, have expressed objections to a center cockpit because it puts the occupants further forward in a wetter part of the boat. However, in five years of cruising in *Tanagra* there was only one day, motor-sailing in the lee of Eleuthera in the Bahamas in a 30- to 35-knot northeaster that kicked up a steep, nasty chop even in the lee, when we might have been more comfortable aft. This is not an important consideration to me if the hull is generally dry, and there are many benefits.

One aspect of center-cockpit boats that I have not been impressed by is the need many people seem to feel for a walk-through from the after cabin to the main cabin. This is used as a big selling point by many designers and builders, but to me it is usually a waste of space that can be better utilized in some other way, and it is seldom vitally needed. There might be a nasty morning or two when dashing through a rainy cockpit to the galley at breakfast time is unpleasant, but that's a low percentage factor.

And so we would have liked another aft-cabin model in our latest boat, but, in adding up all the considerations, we decided that it wasn't the paramount one as long as we had the tricabin layout in some form, and I must admit that the after cockpit in *Brunelle* is very pleasant. It is bigger than a center cockpit would be in a similar size boat, and with a dodger as added protection there is seldom any worry about spray, especially since the hull is a very dry one. There is a good feeling of being near the water, with a better relationship with it than when perched on high in a center cockpit (sometimes, in a steep following sea, it seems almost too close a relationship), but on the minus side, visibility forward is not as good as in a center cockpit.

These are all examples of the constant compromising that goes on in choosing a boat. There were other considerations we had to balance out as well. First, we gave up any idea of racing. The split between racing and cruising is so wide now that it is almost impossible to combine the two and do either of them well. Boats of 60 or 70 feet, or some smaller ones, might still manage this, but not in the size range we wanted. We might go on a club port-to-port race cruise in the cruising canvas class once every few years for the social fun of it, but our racing is confined to one-designs at home. It's much simpler and more rewarding that way, especially when I've never been keen on handicap racing. To me it's aesthetically and psychologically hollow to "beat" a boat whose crew is already ashore and half drunk in the bar by the time you finish. I like to see my competition in the actual position they're in. And all the fuss over rating rules, which started with the first race at Cowes almost two hundred years ago and has never ceased, makes the whole business look rather silly, in my personal opinion. No one is ever really satisfied with a handicap system for long, and it's always a handy excuse for losing.

I know that there are many owners who do want to combine cruising with at least some club racing in Performance Handicap classes, so the need for compromise does exist. It can't be done properly in the Grand Prix IOR boats, but there is a chance to combine performance and comfort for those who want to race in a lower key. The best size for this is in boats under 30 feet, and I'll still take one-design competition as more fun in that league.

In our cruising boat we wanted all the amenities possible, with weight distribution governed by comfort and ease of handling. The bow-chocked anchor, for example, all wrong on a racing boat because of the weight this puts in the bow, is a must when cruising, as far as I'm concerned. Not having to wrestle a mud-caked monster of an anchor over the lifelines and onto the deck (followed by cleanup of the mess), makes a tremendous difference.

Roller-furling sails are another example. Even though they are now well cut and well designed, providing perfectly good cruising performance, they are not racing sails, but there's nothing quite like that zippy roller-shade action for getting rid of the jib when you want to, never leaving the cockpit—and of breaking it out instantly when called for. On this subject, I haven't yet been sold on roller-furling mainsails. They are a wonderful convenience, but there are bugs in them that give me pause. The kind that goes into a slot in the mast and is rolled up inside can bunch up and jam easily if anything gets out of true—I've seen it happen. The ones that furl on a luff wire aft of the mast leave a lot to be desired in windward performance. There are those who say that owners of cruising boats should not be concerned with windward performance, but I still want a boat that will sail well, if not quite to racing standards, on all points. There are times when you're glad she does, either out of sheer fun, or sometimes out of necessity. We ran out of fuel on a long plug across the Mona Passage in *Brunelle* and had to sail the last ten or so miles into San Juan dead to windward in a stiff trade of 18 knots, with a final beat of more than a mile up a narrow channel to Club Nautico. We made it just at twilight, and without good windward performance we would have had an unpleasant time of it. We might not have won a race against an IOR boat over the same distance, and who cares, but the boat was sailing well and doing what we required of her.

This brings up the subject of rig in general. In our favorite size range under 40 feet, I think a divided rig is a waste of time and money. A yawl or ketch looks very salty and all that, but performance suffers on many points, and the added rig and sail means a couple of thousand more dollars at a minimum. I must admit that it has been nice on occasion, in a borrowed ketch, to reach along under jib and jigger in a strong breeze, and those who like to play with a lot of sails can have fun with mizzen staysails and the like. Personally, with roller reefing on the jib (not just roller furling—there's a difference) and the swift simplicity of slab reefing for the main, I don't worry about having to reduce sail when necessary in a single-sticker, and reduced sail inventory means reduced costs.

Originally, roller jibs were meant to be all-or-nothing, as they weren't cut to be used in partial furl except in dire emergencies, but advances have been made that permit partial reefing with roller jibs. Also, we have a cutter rig on *Brunelle*, with a staysail inside the roller reefer, and sail reduction can be very swift indeed with this combination. On a fifty-five-mile passage from Mayaguana to Providenciales, we started with full main and double headrig on a close reach, but the northeast breeze gradually gained heft through the passage until we decided we were lugging too much. In less than five minutes we had the roller reefer rolled up and the main reefed, and she eased along very nicely as the wind continued to increase. (A very special rig, the cat ketch, as on the Sandpiper [p. 89] and the Freedom 40 [p. 134] will be discussed in Part II.)

Draft is important to us because of the shallowness of our home waters, and because of the flexibility a shallow-draft boat provides in such areas as the Bahamas.

The importance of sails was brought home to us in an interesting

*Our Sanderling catboat* Polly, *a minimum cruiser/racer.*

way when we arrived in the Virgin Islands with *Brunelle*. With the CSY fleet of charter boats all around us, this meant that there were other CSY 37s sailing, and we thought it would be instructive to brush with them. We also have a genoa, left over from our old boat, that we had altered to fit the roller-furler stay, and we wanted to see how this sail would affect performance compared to the double headrig. What we didn't realize was that while our sails (made for us by Charles Ulmer) are six-ounce weight with battens and a roach on the main, the charter boats are equipped with nine-ounce sails and roachless, battenless mains to stand up to the rigors of constant charter use. Whenever we got near a charter boat, we breezed by them as though we were an IOR hotshot, and there was no point in trying the genoa. It was very evident what a difference sail cut and weight make. Of course everyone is vaguely aware of that, but this was a graphic example. It's too bad that charter-boat performance has to be affected, and erroneous judgments have probably been formed about the boats' potential, but the economics of charter-boat operation take precedence.

Going below and looking at items other than the accommodation plan, there were a couple of things we'd learned over the years that we felt were important, and again racing considerations would rule them out. CSY offered refrigeration, with a freezer compartment working off the engine, and this is a very pleasant plus. *Tanagra* had a big, well-insulated ice chest, and a hundred-pound bag of crushed ice would last at least a week, even in the Bahamas, but ice can still be a problem in many remote cruising areas, and refrigeration has proved its worth. The engine must be run at least an hour a day to operate the compressor; it is only twelve-volt, so it cannot be hooked up to shore power, but this is the compromise you make, the price you pay, for a delightful convenience. From what we have heard of units that have their own motor, there are a lot more headaches involved than in our relatively simple set-up.

Cooking with pressure alcohol was one of Jane's big bugaboos in *Tanagra*. She approached mealtime with a chip on her shoulder and the language emerging from the galley as she tried to get the alcohol burners to light, after an arduous session of pumping up pressure, would have done credit to a bosun's mate. It was also a limiting system and results often were spotty. This time we have propane, with a carefully engineered system of cutoff valves, safety switches, etc. (the tanks are located under the helmsman's seat and vented through the transom), and all is now happiness in the galley. Cooking is under control, with instant flame at the burner; the oven is useful and efficient; and I have a happy cook as a shipmate. In rough going like the Crooked Island, Caicos, and Mona Passages, she cooked full dinners and breakfasts with no difficulty except the usual personal balancing act, and morale was high on board.

As to the engine, this isn't much of a decision in choosing a boat anymore, as diesel is almost universally the choice (few manufacturers even offer gas in boats over 30 feet) until you get down to the size range where an outboard is big enough to handle the auxiliary's job—or to save a lot of money in installation costs. The initial higher cost in diesel, and the slightly added weight factor, are not real deterrents against the increased safety, reliability, and, at least in some areas, availability of fuel. The latter, of course, is subject to forces beyond an owner's control, and subject to change day by day. The cost saving in diesel fuel, which used to be big, is no longer a significant factor.

All these items were added together while we were making our choice of a boat, and perhaps the final clincher, since there are quite a few boats that could be adapted to our special requirements, was quality of construction. This is a difficult item for the average buyer to determine. A lot must be taken on faith and hearsay, as it is difficult for the layman to look at fiberglass construction and be certain that it is solid and properly done. The serious customer can go into thickness of mat, lay-up methods, bonding procedures between hull and deck, and other important considerations, but most of these are hard to check on without technical knowledge. Unless construction is so shoddy that it hits you in the face (and auxiliary functions like joiner work, seating of fittings, size and quality of hardware, and strength of hatches can be telltale indicators), fiberglass construction can be glossed up fairly easily.

We cruised on two different CSY 44s and everything we could see about them spoke of rugged construction, quality equipment, and careful engineering. A clincher was the experience, documented in photos, of a 44 that had been trapped in the Baths, a rocky, boulder-strewn beach area in the Virgin Islands, through mishandling by a bareboat charterer. Although she pounded on the rocks in the surf for most of a day, the only damage sustained by the time she was pulled off was to rudder and propeller. Only solid construction could stand up to that experience, and it confirmed an opinion we had arrived at without technical backup.

All this may sound like a commercial for CSY, but I raise these points merely to show the reasons behind a specific choice. There are many well-built, well-conceived cruising boats, and I'm sure we would have been pleased with quite a few. You can only buy one boat at a time though, and all the above was behind the reasoning that went into our decision.

I should say a word here about hull form. Anyone who has read my writings over the years knows that I am not partial to multihulls as cruising boats, and I have received a goodly number of poison-pen letters as a result (multihull devotees are fanatics, I can assure you). I admit that trimarans and catamarans have made long ocean passages, including circumnavigations and rounding Cape Horn, and have gotten away with it. And I will admit that multihulls have certain advantages: they are cheaper to build and have more space per dollar than most cruising boats. On certain points of sailing in certain conditions they can be fast, although on the average the multihulls that one sees cruising are generally not fast because they are usually overloaded and poorly rigged. I have seen beautifully appointed multihulls that make wonderful charter boats when used in the right circumstances, and I do believe that they have their place.

I also believe, however, that they are not safe or practical for offshore passaging because they can capsize and not be righted, and poorly built ones are dangerous in not being properly stressed in the bracing between the hulls. As a minor complaint, they are awkward to handle in close quarters, and if all boats were multihulls, marinas would have a terrible problem in providing slips.

To me, a good cruising hull should be a monohull with a relatively long keel and attached rudder, or skeg rudder, that will settle in a groove and track well without excessive helming. It should have good

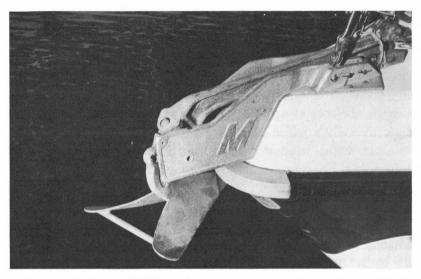

*A bow-chocked plow (CQR) anchor is our answer to the anchor problem.*

beam for stability and room below decks, a good entry and flared bow for dryness, and a generally sea-kindly, stable feel with a slow, gentle motion in a seaway (as opposed to a cranky, jerky boat with a fin keel that must be steered like a skittish dinghy at all times). I'm pleased with *Brunelle,* but I can also say that I think the Ray Hunt Concordias are a classic example of what I am talking about. The Concordia hull seems to fit the water perfectly and naturally, with a delightful ease of motion, and the sailing qualities have certainly been proved many times. The contrast between steering this kind of hull and having to fight the constant skittishness and unpredictable orneriness of the light, short-keeled spade-rudder type that has become popular in ocean racing has to be felt to be believed.

Another item over which I disagree with a great many people is the need for a navigation station. It seems to me that a great amount of space is wasted in paying obeisance to the questionable need for this item that could be used to better advantage. I know there are owners who love to act like Merlin at his crystal ball, twisting dials and performing incantations and mumbo-jumbo in the sacred precincts of the navigation station, but I think this function is vastly overrated in cruising boats. In an ocean racer, yes, where pinpoint navigation is a part of tactics and strategy, but there isn't that much time spent on cruising navigation, except in long offshore passages. In charter boats, where night navigation is prohibited and most operations are within visual sighting of the next objective, navigation stations are unnecessary, and even on boats that have them, I find that I prefer to have the chart in the cockpit with me, and the table in the main cabin does perfectly well for laying out courses.

I know that in some quarters this thinking is considered equally as heinous as being against motherhood, but it is just an opinion I have developed in fifty years of cruising.

I've been discussing our size range, but there are naturally many buyers who have requirements different from ours. When we were in a tighter financial situation twenty years ago, with tuition bills high on the budget, we were delighted with a 24-footer that suited a growing family. When the tuition factor became even higher, we went down to an 18-foot catboat for a while, a minimum cruising boat if there ever was one, but we like her so much that we still have her for day sailing and racing around home, while *Brunelle* takes us to more distant waters.

One of the key factors in choosing a boat, especially in the smaller ranges, is to make sure that the designer and builder haven't tried to do too much with a given size. When you have 24-footers that sleep six, or full headroom in a 20-footer, something has to give. One summer we had the use of an outboard-powered 22-foot cabin cruiser that was billed as a "four-sleeper." Technically she did have four bunks, although my feet hung out quite a way over the bottom, but there was no room left for stowage—even for a toothbrush. The "four-sleeper" pitch may have been a selling point, but the boat was unusable as such.

In smaller auxiliaries, there are many ways to make efficient use of space to avoid the above sort of nonsense, and they are worth looking for. On our 24-foot Amphibi-Ette *Mar Claro,* as you will see (p. 64), we had a convertible hood that solved the headroom problem and actually added a great deal to effective cockpit space, and there are later developments of pop-tops, expanding hatches, and the like that are a help. Most of them have drawbacks in watertight integrity or ease of handling, and once again we are in the area of compromise.

*The CSY 37 cutter* Brunelle, *our choice to fit our requirements.*

There might be some who say that our tricabin layout in 37-foot *Brunelle* is contrary to the dictum of not trying to do too much, and there are many boats as big as 40 or 42 feet where this would be true, but designer Peter Schmitt thought the problems out, and the result is functional.

In small boats, we have seen ingenious use of slide-away galleys, and double use of space can make a great difference in some cases. I have already mentioned outboard power for small auxiliaries as a cost saver on initial installation, but another plus is in space saving. Inboard engines take up a big percentage of cubic footage in boats under 30–32 feet, and the amount freed for other uses is important (The relatively new sail-drive engines overcame this latter objection quite, handily).

In larger boats, the engine installation is another item to look at carefully. Space may be saved by some artful tucking away of the power plant, but this can often mean that no one but a double-jointed midget can work on the engine, and there aren't too many of them around. Sometimes the engine is stashed away so securely that the block can't be removed from the boat for overhauling or repowering without major dismantling of the superstructure or cockpit. This can mean real trouble, but an owner is steadily concerned with routine maintenance and should not have to stand on his head or do a double backbend simply to check the lube oil. Somehow it also often seems that this sort of installation has been poorly engineered in other ways and ends up needing more attention than the comfortably accessible one.

Another failing designers are prone to, especially in boats under 30 feet, is to make them scaled-down models of much larger boats. They may look shippy and graceful, but long ends, a narrow beam, and a low profile combine into a very uncomfortable little boat—pleasing to look at perhaps, but hell to be in. The other side of this coin is the practice of ignoring looks and ending up with a misshapen boat, all out of proportion, just so she can have headroom, an enclosed head, or whatever. Not only are they ungainly to look at, they are often cranky to handle, with poor stability.

How a boat looks has always added greatly to its appeal to a romantically inclined buyer. It's certainly nice to have a boat that is handsome as long as beauty devolves from function, but many a purchase has been made on the strength of looks alone, with no regard to practicality. Looks have always had a relatively low position on my priority list in choosing a boat, and I honestly have to admit that there have been better looking boats we could have chosen in the same size range each time, but function and practicality have their own appeal. As the old saying goes, "Handsome is as handsome does."

Choosing a cruising auxiliary is a subject that has endless ramifications. Thinking about it can often keep a dreamer busy for years before a decision is reached, and there are some who really don't want to go beyond this stage—dreaming is enough. Others ardently await the day when their finances will allow putting all the dreams and analysis into a final decision. They go on this way for weeks, months, or years, and finally decide. Then the real fun begins.

# Commissioning

Once the decision has been made and the money plunked down, the next phase of owning an auxiliary is commissioning, and this is something most buyers don't give a great deal of thought to until they are face to face with it. Of course, in the financial aspects of planning the purchase it is an absolute imperative to allow for a lot more expenditures before the boat is ready to operate (and operating costs—insurance, dockage, fuel, maintenance, repairs—must be figured in too, perhaps balanced against reduced outlay for what was formerly spent on other forms of recreation and vacation travel).

What you are doing is virtually establishing another household, as equipping a cruising sailboat is at least as complicated as setting up an apartment, with some nautical extras that no household needs. The list grows to amazing proportions, and the multitude of details that must be attended to is staggering. Fortunately, it is all a lot of fun and kind of exciting—if you have allowed enough for the financial shock.

Commissioning a boat is a rather personal operation. Each one is a bit different, and each owner's tastes and requirements differ, so most advice has to be along general lines. Rather than that, let's go through the commissioning of *Brunelle* as an example of what to expect, and what, to some extent, must be done, for every boat.

The process with her was a bit unusual, as CSY does not have dealers and sales are direct from the factory, with delivery taken there and commissioning carried out there. This is in contrast to buying through a dealer and doing the job with him, usually closer to the owner's home, so that the owner can remain in touch for a period of time and make sure that everything has been done right. At CSY, once commissioning is through at their Tampa plant, most boats are taken out of the area, and it is a bit harder to check back and have omissions corrected.

The reverse of this is that, in commissioning at the plant, you are with experts who really know the boat and have been with her since she was started (you can't really talk about "laying keels" anymore). The commissioning operation has been refined to a science, and it is relatively easy to have corrections or alterations made right at the source. And no matter who builds a boat, or how careful and well-thought-out all their procedures are, it's a fact of life—and no criticism of a manufacturer—that an item as complicated and sophisticated as a cruising auxiliary is bound to have some items that need fixing when she first comes off the production line. The old gag about not buying a new car that was produced on a Monday points up the human factor in putting together something this complex, and human errors can be made by even the most careful workmen. It might almost be a maxim along the lines of the Detroit gag not to buy a boat that was finished on a Friday afternoon. Someone in a hurry to get off the job just might leave little touches unfinished, and little touches make a great deal of difference in a sailing yacht.

CSY has a factory sales force, and each customer has his personal shepherd for the commissioning process. Ours was Ford King, whom we happened to have known in a previous reincarnation as a magazine publisher. He thought he was taking on a nice quiet semiretirement job at CSY and ended up working like someone sending warships to the fleet in World War II. Actually, his thoughtfulness and understanding added greatly to the fun as he guided us through item after item, and his familiarity with the problems was a big help.

The commissioning process really begins well before the boat is delivered. In the previous chapter I talked about the broad subjects and categories that have to be covered in making the choice of a boat as to rig, layout, draft, power plant, and other basics. Then, once the choice is made on those considerations, comes the getting down to details on any number of items. After placing our order in March 1978, we had a preliminary session at CSY on such items as hull color, sails, upholstery and decor, choices of basic equipment such as radio and electronic instruments that had to be installed during construction, and other options to do with things like portholes that had to be decided before construction started.

Hull color was a special item. CSY had established a "trademark" color scheme for its boats of beige topsides and maroon sheer stripe, but with the 37 as a new model, they weren't yet sure about what they would be offering with it. The prototype hull had been a dark, fisherman green, handsome and traditional, but added thought brought the decision that it was too dark for tropical use. While the subject was still open, I asked for the same color we had had on our Amphibi-Ette and Morgan OI 36, a pale-blue topsides. This has come to be known in some quarters as *Weatherly* blue after the 1962 America's Cup defender (but we had it on *Mar Claro* in 1958, and we've liked it ever since for both aesthetic and practical reasons). It doesn't fade like a darker color, it hides stains better than white, and it is a handsome color on the water, blending nicely. We got our request, but soon thereafter the decision was made at CSY to stick to one basic color scheme without offering options, and therefore we have a one-of-a-kind hull decor as far as CSY boats are concerned. Sometimes you do have this option as a buyer. Usually, in stock boats the builder doesn't offer a choice, and what you get is most often white. Afterward, if you feel like spending the money, you can always arrange for a customized color job via one of the new miracle paints.

There are usually some questions about deck hardware and fittings that should be settled as early as possible, but this varies widely of course with different manufacturers, and with whether the order is being placed before construction starts or a finished boat is being bought off a showroom floor. If options are available for things like pulpits, steering systems, rig variations (double headrig or single; single stick or divided rig), winches, anchor handling, cockpit cushions, Bimini top or other awnings, dodger, or extra hatches, for example, early decisions are helpful for a smooth flow of materials and equipment into the construction. It is possible, though, to have them added later, in most cases.

We went for options such as extra ports from cockpit to galley and after cabin (and are glad we did for ventilation, light, and convenience of passing items back and forth), gates in the lifelines on both sides of the boat, self-tailing winches, a dodger and Bimini, boom gallows frame, masthead and spreader halyards, cockpit cushions, roller-reefing

*The Flasher, also known by other names by other sailmakers, is a big help in downwind cruising.*

jib, and the double headrig, to name a few, and after experience with using them we don't regret any of them as being unnecessary. (We did not go for a carved name board for the transom.)

One extra that I'm delighted we decided on was a special sail known as a Flasher, made by Charles Ulmer, who made our sails for *Brunelle.* This is a "poleless spinnaker" for downwind work. It looks and acts like a spinnaker but tacks to the stem, with a collar holding its pennant close to the forestay, instead of being rigged to a pole with guy, lift, foreguy, and all those racing-machine trappings. It works beautifully in winds up to 16 knots or so with the wind anywhere from broad on the quarter to just forward of the beam, and really adds to

44

*In southern waters, a Bimini top is a must for sun protection.*

performance, not to mention adding a touch of color. In ordering ours, I selected just about every hue in the rainbow for the rather narrow panels.

It does not draw when dead before the wind, and since it's a big sail it could give trouble if the breeze pipes up, but two people, one on the halyard and one to trim when it's being set and to gather in at the bow when it's being doused, can handle it easily. And someone has to be on the helm, of course. Other sailmakers call the same sort of sail by their own pet names, and I recommend it highly for adding spice to cruising under sail.

As someone who has had his share of back troubles in the advancing years (who hasn't, it would seem), I ordered a power windlass for the anchor, but this turned out to be something of a luxury. The bow-chocked plow anchor is such a handy installation to work that we haven't used the windlass much, but it is there in case the skipper should come down with the back bends.

Which gets us to electronics, and the next set of choices to be made during commissioning. I have had a personal theory, shared by many, which we might refer to as "Robinson's law": the more gadgets there are on a boat, the more items there are to go wrong, requiring repairs and expenditures, plus causing a nuisance. Two years of sub-chaser duty in World War II did much to fortify this theory, as I don't remember a time when absolutely everything was simultaneously in working order, and nothing I have seen since has changed it. In our Amphibi-Ette we purposely got along without a water system, as we figured plastic water bottles were easy to handle and were more flexible for filling and stowing, and there wasn't the temptation for the younger generation to play with faucets.

Things are a bit more complicated when you go from 24 to 37 feet and intend to live aboard for long periods at a time, but our basic approach was still to keep things as simple as possible. Although I gather improvements have been made, bringing a greater degree of reliability, we had had unsatisfactory experiences with fancy digital logs and depth sounders and decided to have a direct-reading depth sounder only, and no speed or wind instruments. Some people feel lost without them, and ocean racers can't function without them anymore, but to me they are items that simply tend to fail when you want them most in cruising boats. (And I would just as soon *not* have had the one working in the Bermuda Race one year when it hit the top of the scale at eighty and jammed there a few times!) Items like this are a matter of personal taste and inclination as much as anything. So far, we haven't had too much trouble estimating boat speed for D.R. purposes. It all depends on what you like to play with. An autopilot would be a nice luxury, but far from a necessity with us.

I feel pretty much the same way about radio as about other electronics, and in the five years we had *Tanagra* I managed to make exactly one transmission. We were berthed at South Street Seaport in New York; I was alone on board and didn't want to leave the boat untended with a great many people all around, so I called my office on VHF instead of walking down the pier to a pay phone. We did use it to listen to the weather broadcasts.

We still wanted to have VHF, however, and I must admit that we have used it fairly frequently in *Brunelle*, especially down through the islands. In the Caicos VHF is like a party line, with all sorts of chatter between boats and to marinas and shore facilities, and the same is true in the Virgins. Because we intended to go to regions of the Caribbean where VHF would be ineffective, we decided to add single sideband too. In the first year I didn't make one transmission on it, and it has been of very little help in picking up weather broadcasts, but it does mean that we have the potential to stay in touch in even the remotest areas.

I was interested in Loran, but Loran C had not been established for the Caribbean areas we were heading for, so we didn't order it. It would be great to have, and a wider range is in the works for it. For an RDF, we have found a portable one to suffice, although accuracy down to a fine fix is not really possible. All these items are, again, a matter of personal choice and, very definitely, finances.

There wasn't much question about ordering mechanical refrigeration. CSY offers the type of system in which the compressor runs off the main engine, so you must run the engine for at least an hour a day to keep the refrigeration working, but this is only a nuisance when you are staying in a marina for a few days, and it is a relatively simple system that has few bugs. In an area where ice is always available, a well-insulated box should do the trick and help keep things simple, but it's nice to have refrigeration in areas where ice is a problem, and we were heading for them. This system does not work off 110-volt shore power, which would be a plus, but that would involve more complications.

We did order a shore-power converter as an extra so that when in a marina we could to be assured of all the electricity we wanted without worrying about the batteries, and in fact charging them up via the converter. We have a toaster and a vacuum cleaner (and, I hesitate to admit, a TV) that only work on 110 volts, and and having shore power available is a major plus.

I won't go into the thorny problem of heads. Anyone who has read any of my editorials in *Yachting* over the years knows what I think about the idiotic requirements for treatment on boats intended for offshore use and long-range cruising, and as of this writing I have not found an approved system that is any good at all. New boats are required to have treatment or holding-tank systems built in, and we had to pay for an expensive installation that we find completely useless. Suffice it to say that after leaving the builder's yard we were able to have it bypassed for operations outside U.S. waters, where the stupid regulations are not in effect. In U.S. waters, our boat can quickly be reconverted to legal status. Enough said. Because it's such a ridiculous situation, I have no recommendations.

All these decisions were made before any work was done on the boat. They were commissioning details in that they didn't have to be made until the order was signed. Once work started, we began to think about all the rest of the stuff that must go aboard before a boat can be said to be in commission. We had piles of personal gear that could be transferred from *Tanagra*, but there was a lot of new stuff to think about too. Here you are into everything from foul-weather gear to clothes pins, from bed linen to signal flags, from carving knives to hibachis. We took a carload of gear from *Tanagra* to *Brunelle* and still had to range the stores of Tampa and St. Petersburg for all sorts of items. Fortunately, when we sold *Tanagra* to a company running bareboat charters out of Nassau, much of the personal gear did not have to go with her, as well as major items like the rubber dinghy, and our children gave us handsome unbreakable, nonskid dinnerware and cups decorated with burgees and the boat's name. Still, we went through a long list of housekeeping and boatkeeping items.

We would suddenly remember that a swimming ladder was not provided and had to shop for one, and the standard docking and "safety package" that came with the boat had to be augmented with extra life jackets, mooring lines, fenders, and an extra anchor. Also, we decided that the twenty-five-pound plow anchor provided as standard was not big enough for our intended use so we added a thirty-five-pounder to the list. We debated getting an outboard for the Avon inflatable, but decided against having any gas aboard. (The CSY 37 has no after deck, where many owners keep their gas cans, so stowage would be a problem.

In general, though, we just didn't want the problem, and rowing has been good for us, with no major inconvenience so far.)

All this material was collected while the boat was going through her final stages at the plant, and it took several days to put it aboard. As we worked, we made stowage lists for each locker, drawer, and cupboard, and it was amazing how many places there were for tucking things away. In a common mistake, we were optimistic in putting stuff in the bilge drops that should have been kept in drier places, but finally most of the gear was well and properly stowed, and we make every effort to return everything to the same spot when we finish using it.

Despite the time spent, there were things we had forgotten, and each port along the way in our shakedown cruise saw us coming up with more items. For example, we hadn't thought of a fly swatter until we got into warm weather in the lower Bahamas and farther south and needed one, and then we couldn't find one anywhere in the stores. It became a joke that no hardware or supermarket in the Bahamas, Turks and Caicos, Dominican Republic, or Puerto Rico seemed to have fly swatters, until we finally found one on the tiny, isolated island of Culebra off Puerto Rico.

All this was a great part of the fun of starting out with a new cruising boat. As I have said, this was all a personalized experience dealing with one boat—our own—and details will differ by owner and by boat type. I hope, though, that you've gotten the general idea.

### Recommended Equipment List For Cruising Boats

Anchor rodes, 150', 5/8"
  Nylon, 2
Anchors
Ammeter
Anemometer, pocket
Ashtrays, beanbag
Awning, Dacron, cockpit
Batteries, 2 sets of 2, 12V

Battery, switch
Bilge pump, hand
Binoculars, 7 × 50
Blankets, Dacron for all
  bunks
Boat hook
Bow chock, mahogany, and
  roller for anchor

Brushes
  Long-handled
  Scrub
  Whisk broom
Chafing gear on lines
Charcoal grill
Clothes hangers
Clothespins
Compass
Courtesy flags
Cushions, cockpit
Cushions, life preserver, 4–6
Dishcloths, 2
Dish locker
Dock lines
Dynaplates
Electric bonding system
Fenders
Fire extinguisher
First-aid kit
Fishing rods, reels, and line
Flares, hand, emergency
Flashlights, 3
Flippers, masks, and snorkels
Flyswatter
Fog bell
Fuel filter
Fuel measuring stick
Funnel, fuel, with strainer
Funnel, water
Galley equipment
  Beer-can opener, stainless
    steel
  Butter box and cover
  Chore Girls
  Coffeepot

Corkscrew
Double boiler and lid
Frying pan
Funnel, plastic
Glasses
Ice pick
Insulated glasses, coffee, 6
Juice container and top,
    36-oz.
Juice container and top,
    50-oz.
Juice squeezer
Knife, large
Knives, paring, 2
Plates, 8", 6
Plates, 10", 6
Soup bowls, 6
Mixing bowls, large
Mixing bowls, small
Peeler
Potholders, 2
Sponges, cellulose, 2; galley, 2
Sugar bowl
Tableware, 6 each knives,
    forks, teaspoons,
    tablespoons, stainless steel
Toaster
Turner
Utensil box
Genoa sheet gear, including
    track and fair-lead blocks
Ice bag
Insect repellent
International navigation lights
Jerry jugs for extra water
Lead line

Life preservers, horseshoe and
    bracket
Light bulbs, extra
Lightning grounding system
Mattresses, seat cushions on
    each bunk
Mirror, head
Mooring cleats
Mop, cellulose
Navigation gear
    Necessary charts
    Dividers
    Parallel rulers
    Pencils
Oars and oarlocks for skiff
Oil-pressure gauge
Outboard motor on skiff
Pillowcases
Pillows, foam
Radiotelephone
Roller-reefing gear for jib
Roller reefing, main boom
Screens

Scuppers (through-deck)
Sheets for berths
Signal horn
Skiff
Stern pole and ensign
Strainer, fuel
Swimming ladder
Tool kit
    Extra fuses
    Nuts and bolts
    Nylon cord
    Plastic tape
    Tool set
Towels, supply of large and
    medium
Tow rope, 1/2" polypropylene,
    for skiff
Valves, fuel shut-off
Ventilators, engine-room to
    meet CG requirements
Washcloths
Wind scoop, Dacron on forward
    hatch for hyperventilation

# Thoughts on Bareboating

~~~~~~~~~~~~~~~~~~~~~~~~~~~~~~~~~~~~~~~~~~~~~~~

Since so many people are now doing a major part of their cruising, or at least their major adventure away from home waters, in the southern bareboat charter fleets, a word might be in order about this late-blooming and fast-growing phenomenon of the cruising world. In 1966, when we went on our first bareboat charter out of St. Thomas in the Virgin Islands, there were only eleven boats available, operating out of Dick Avery's Boat House. A dozen years later there were hundreds of boats, with more being added all the time, in the American and British Virgins, with many more in the Bahamas, the west coast of Florida, the Windwards and Leewards, the Bay Islands of Honduras, the South Pacific, Greece, Denmark, Sardinia, and Australia.

For bareboating, they range from little two-berth 22-footers to 50-foot ketches, with the vast majority in the 32- to 41-foot range, although a trend to bigger boats was becoming stronger in the late 1970s, with 44-, 45-, and 46-footers being offered.

Choosing a bareboat is quite different from choosing your own private, personal vessel. First of all, you can afford a much bigger boat for one or two weeks of chartering than you could for your own owner-ship, especially if the cost is being split among two or more couples. This is a very common practice and is a good idea if you choose your companions wisely. There has to be basic agreement on the type of sailing to be done, the division of labor among the galley slaves, and the amount of partying and carousing to be expected. Compatability in all these is vital. Some couples who are great friends for Saturday night partying at the country club might not wear well during a longer and more intimate relationship.

As for the boat, the choice, starting with finances, comes down to the number of people she will accommodate comfortably (not just "sleep"), and the demands she will make on the sailing skills of the

*A fleet of bareboats on turnaround at Road Town, Tortola, British Virgins.*

charterers. A boat big enough to take three couples in privacy may be too big to handle if there is only one competent sailor in the crowd—but the more privacy the better. (See "Choosing a Boat" and my remarks about separate heads with the staterooms—these considerations are even more important for the smooth working of a joint charter, and the need for privacy increases noticeably with the age of the parties involved, especially the women.)

If the charter party is a family with growing children as part of the crowd, then privacy is not half as important as the total number of bunks. Auxiliary gear like diving equipment could mean more in this case. When adult couples are involved, a good rule of thumb would be to stick to a single couple in boats under 30 feet unless the general age is still pretty youthful and everyone knows everyone well. From 30 to 40 feet, two couples should be plenty, as a third couple will have to sleep in one of the open cabins and everyone will be on top of everyone else in the awkward periods of getting up, going to bed, and getting meals. When they are over 40 feet, many of the charter yachts do have room for three couples without too much of the elbow-in-the-eye sort of thing, especially awkward when it's someone else's elbow in your wife's eye. Still, there has to be a good understanding, and, as a reminder, the boat is much more to handle. Anchoring always seems to be the main problem and the cause of more bickering on the bareboats we have observed.

Most bareboat fleets have standardized their boats and equipment so that repairs and replacements can easily be effected, and the between-charters cleanup is much easier when everything is the same. For this reason, most of the boats have all the individuality and charm of motel rooms. Everything is efficient and functional, and each item has been thought out for its special use, but there is a minimum of character. Also, sails tend to be of heavy cloth, with battenless, roachless mainsails for utility's sake, and performance may not be what you would have in a personally owned boat of the same type. This can vary considerably among the different companies in the business, but bareboats are usually not the best advertisements for a design's capabilities and potential.

Some operators have even put reduced rigs on their fleet boats, especially in areas of generally heavy winds, and usually this is a wise idea, making for greater stability and ease of handling. All of this means that, should your intention be to beat everybody in sight, you'd be better off in the Bermuda Race than on a bareboat charter.

Many of the boats whose plans will be shown in Part II were designed for, or have been adapted to, bareboat chartering, and that's the way I got to sail them. It took me a while to get used to the difference between sailing a charter boat and sailing my own, and all of us who use them should always remember that.

The various cruising areas will be described in Part III, but it might help to have a rundown here, very broadly and generally rating the areas by degree of challenge and sophistication for the charterer, remembering that normal conditions are not always what you may get in any given week. We've been to plenty of areas where we were told "This *never* happens here. You should have been here last week." The rating is based on the average of conditions, the difficulty (or ease) of piloting, and the general lay of the land. From easiest up (and not going into overseas areas) they are: the Virgins, the Abacos, the west coast of Florida and the Keys, the big islands of the Lesser Antilles, the Grenadines, and the Bay Islands of Honduras. This should be used only as a rough guide, both for those who feel somewhat inexperienced and for the real salts who want the most challenge they can get. None is absolutely "easy" or "difficult." All are very well adapted to bareboating and have tremendous rewards for sailors.

# Part II

## Cruising Boats

The boats discussed and analyzed here have two things in common. They are all intended for cruising under sail, in most cases with a big assist from auxiliary power, and I have had some personal experience with all of them. Some I have owned, some I have cruised in extensively and more than once, some I have chartered, some I have borrowed, and some I have just been in for a short sail, but I do have personal knowledge of all of them. Many excellent cruising boats have naturally been left out under this method of selection, and inclusion here does not automatically mean a recommendation. As you will note, I have tried to bring out both the weak and the strong points of each boat in an effort to show what works and what does not, and what I think represents good and not-so-good thinking. Many of these boats are no longer in production and could only be obtained secondhand, so this is not a "buyer's guide." It is a guide to the many elements, the compromises and choices, that go toward making a successful cruising boat, and I have included older boats as an example of a certain type of thinking, often an innovation, if not a breakthrough, that has had an influence on later designs. (Sometimes their accommodation plan and sail profile are no longer available.) There are also boats from abroad, from Europe and Australia, that are not available in other areas, but again they can serve as an indication of practices and ways of thinking that are of interest to all who are caught up in the question of what the best boat is for them—to own, to charter, or perhaps to dream about for a few more years.

# The Sanderling Catboat

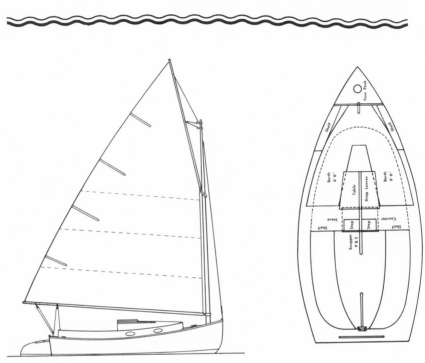

*The Sanderling 18-foot catboat.* 18½" × 17'9" × 8'6" × 1'7"

The catboat concept probably offers the most cubic feet of usable space per foot of overall length of any small cruising boat, and it is a wonderful compromise until the sail area becomes too big for efficient and safe handling. I would say that 18 to 22 feet is the ideal range for catboats to be used for cruising. Over that, if you happen to be caught in a squall or in an increasing wind on a run, handling the sail can be anything from a problem to impossible.

Our 18-foot catboat *Polly* is a Sanderling, the class name given to the specific model developed by Breck Marshall of South Dartmouth, Massachusetts, who also designed a 22-footer on the same principles. He took the classic Cape Cod cat, a design going back to the early nineteenth century, and adapted it to modern materials. The weakness of the old Cape Cod cat, which was designed for offshore fishing single-handed out of the shallow bays of the cape, was in the weight of the solid wooden mast placed right in the bow. This required a broad, flat bow to support the mast, and thus the boats were poor to windward. Also, the weight of the telephone pole mast made them root and broach on a run or broad reach, causing a heavy, sometimes impossible, weather helm. By using a hollow aluminum mast, Marshall could make the bow much finer, with hollowed sections, and the Sanderling's windward performance is very good. Downwind control has also been improved, and the Sanderling is a lively, able sailer. She can take rough seas better than most boats her size.

As an 18-footer, she has cabin accommodations equal to many 22-footers, with sitting headroom, a head, and a shelf that can be used for a portable stove. There is stowage under the bunks, and shelves could be added above them for more stowage if desired. Water bottles and an ice chest have to be portable but can fit under the cockpit seats, and lamps and running lights are also portable and self-contained.

A six-horsepower outboard is about right for power. Bigger than that, the power is wasted, and the motor is too hard to manhandle on and off the bracket. We have used a four-horsepower motor with perfectly adequate performance, perhaps a half knot less than boats with a six, and it is a joy to handle on and off the bracket and to stow under a cockpit seat or on the cabin sole when not in use.

For camp cruising in areas like Cape Cod, Great South Bay, Barnegat, the Chesapeake, and the Florida Keys and Florida west coast, this kind of boat makes a lot of sense, and I would love to have one in the Exumas some day for the ultimate in gunkholing.

There are two sets of reef points. It is not all that easy to put in a reef while underway because of the long overhang of the boom beyond the transom, but once a reef is in she handles like a baby. I have only had a double reef once, in about a 30-knot breeze, and again she handled beautifully.

Some modernists look askance at a gaff rig, but it makes much more sense with the mast right in the bow, where no shrouds are

*The Sanderling 18-foot catboat.*

possible. Also, there is the old-fashioned advantage of "scandalizing" the sail by dropping the peak if a sudden emergency arises, reducing the sail area by one-third.

In our home club, the Sanderling is raced as a one-design and provides extremely even competition, and there are extra dividends in comfortable day sailing, supper parties and picnics under sail, over-nighting, and cruising. For family camp cruising, a cockpit tent can be rigged to make bunk space out of the cockpit seats. Our club members have ranged as far as Cape Cod and the Chesapeake in their boats.

61

# The Chrysler 22

I first came across this boat in its prototype stage when I worked with a TV camera crew making an instructional movie on how to sail, using the plywood prototype of the design as the boat in question. Just about everything was wrong with it at that stage, and it was fascinating to sail a production model a few months later to see how the bugs had been taken out of her. As first turned out as a one-off prototype, she was very badly balanced, with a heavy weather helm in any kind of puff and a lee helm in light air. She was also very unstable and skittish—all in all a bad boat.

Halsey Herreshoff, the third-generation representative of the famous yacht design family, was her designer, and he obviously went "back to the drawing board" and corrected the early faults.

The rig was shortened a bit, ballast was added, and the rudder size and shape were changed. The result was a boat that felt entirely different when she went into production. It was a lesson to me in how the little things that are not obvious to the layman can make a great difference in a boat. The end result is a smart and able little cruising boat that sails like a one-design racer but has been well set up for cruising. This is not a boat to head for the South Pacific in, or even to spend an uninterrupted two-week vacation cruise in (unless you are young and very adaptable), but for overnighting, weekending, and limited cruising, she makes great use of her size.

Double use of space is one of the keys to her success, with generously large bunks also serving as settees, and an ingenious tuck-away galley that slides in and out of a quarter berth area and is completely out of the way when not needed. The ice chest is portable and can be moved to the handiest spot. An outboard on a bracket for auxiliary power keeps the rest of the boat free of machinery, the best solution in this size range, although the sail-drive concept of a motor of out-

*The Chrysler 22.* 22' × 19' × 7'9" × 4'6"

board configuration permanently installed in the interior of the boat is increasing in popularity in even the smallest cruising boats. It does add to initial cost, of course, although it is not as expensive as a conventional inboard installation.

With an adjustable keel, not really a conventional centerboard, the Chrysler 22 is well adapted to trailing, and this is one of the major advantages of a boat of this size. There is a practical range for it far wider than for a bigger boat that has to proceed to distant waters on its own bottom. The owner of a trailable can take in relatively exotic distant waters and change the scene at will in the course of a conventional vacation, while the bigger boat is in effect confined to home waters.

# The Amphibi-Ette

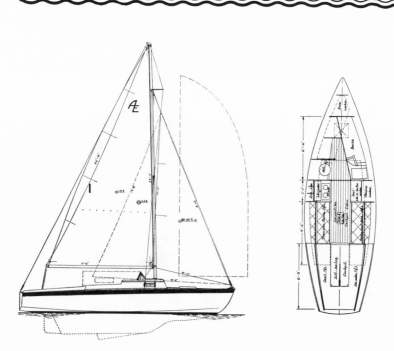

*The 24-foot Amphibi-Ette.* 24'1" × 20'1" × 7'9" × 2'4"

This 24-footer, smallest of the Controversy type promoted in the 1950s by Farnham Butler and Cy Hamlin of Mount Desert Island, Maine, was the first cruising boat I owned, launched in March 1958, and I literally wrote a book about her (*New Boat,* published in 1961 and long since out of print). I don't propose to do that again here, but she did have a lot of interesting, and at the time innovative, features (and incidentally, her fourth owner was going strong with her entering the 1980s).

We owned *Mar Claro* for nine years and she suited us well at the time, both financially and nautically. Our children were in their teens and all five of us could manage to fit into her at the same time, with the three females tripling up in the very ample double bunk forward. She was trailable and we were at an adventurous age, taking her to the Great Lakes, Maine, southern New England, Florida, and the Bahamas, mostly on the strength of her trailability.

It was the idea of Butler, who conceived and promoted her, and Hamlin, who did the specifics of the design, to produce a light-displacement, trailable boat that would be inexpensive (since weight governs the price of a boat to a very large extent), and much roomier than conventional boats her size through the use of reverse sheer and a convertible cabin hood. (This type was called Controversy because the ideas were contrary to tradition.) Since conventionally planked wooden boats that needed caulking and dried out when out of water were not adaptable to trailing, she had to be of seamless construction (this was in prefiberglass days). Her bottom, a rounded hull flaring to a hard chine, was strip-planked, and her topsides were a specially coated plywood. In the nine years we had her she never leaked a drop, and she was no more difficult to maintain than a fiberglass boat since painting her topsides was no more of a problem than keeping a fiberglass boat waxed, and all boats need antifouling on the bottom. The biggest maintenance problem was the canvas hood, which gave her full headroom in the main cabin, and a double cockpit, with or without navy top, in good weather. This tended to deteriorate and had to be replaced twice while we owned her. The modern pop-top used in quite a few boats in this size range is an outgrowth of the Controversy hood.

As I have mentioned, I like to keep equipment as simple as possible, so she had no running water, a Sterno stove, and an icebox compartment that was built to take a portable chest. She was livable if simple, very little ever went wrong, and we spent as much as two weeks at a time in her in adequate comfort. Without the full headroom under the hood, I doubt if we would have wanted to stay aboard this long.

Her keel-centerboard underbody, with a draft of 2 feet 4 inches, allowed real gunkholing, and she was the best boat for the Exumas we've ever been in. She sailed well enough to windward with her keel so that we only used the board when racing. She was fast enough to win her share of races and regattas, including a first in Off Soundings

*The 24-foot Amphibi-Ette* Mar Claro.

once; able enough to handle a 55-knot squall in the Gulf Stream with no difficulty; and stiff in a blow since she was relatively underrigged. On a broad reach in a blow, her chines picked her up on a semiplane, and she could go well over hull speed, often staying with 40-footers boat for boat.

She would look old-fashioned now, despite her reverse sheer, against modern fiberglass slickers, but she was ahead of her time when she was new, and a lot of the ideas in her that were new then have since become accepted as standard.

# The Westerly Tiger

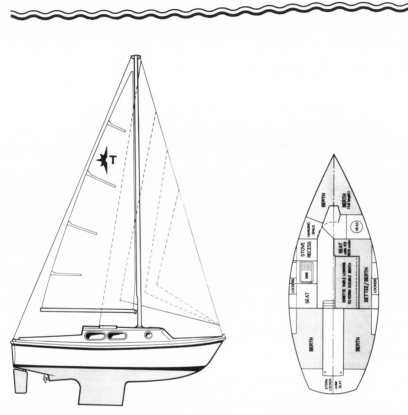

*The 25-foot Westerly Tiger.* 25′1″ × 21′10″ × 8′9″ × 4′3″

My general impression of British boats, especially in the smaller size ranges, has been that they are overgrown dog kennels into which one crawls, usually wearing foul-weather gear, to remain hunched up in a fetal position for most of the cruise, or one sits in a cockpit that is equally poorly adapted to the human body. But the 25-foot Westerly Tiger does a good job of dispelling this impression. The Westerly company has been one of the few foreign builders with an understanding of the needs of the American market, and this early model from

67

*The 25-foot Westerly Tiger.*

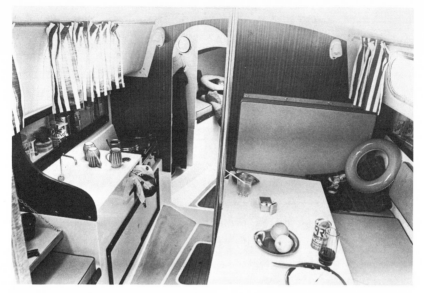

*The 25-foot Westerly Tiger.*

them is a good example. I don't know of many 25-footers, no matter where built, that make better use of available space, and I speak from experience, as I spent a week cruising in one with my son, his wife, and their two young children, and we managed very well. In fact, they spent five summers cruising through Europe in their boat *Shere Khan* (Kipling's tiger, if you don't get the allusion), often with other guests aboard.

Somehow, the boat provides full headroom (my son is 6 feet 2 inches) without seeming ungainly or out of proportion, although she does have a very generous freeboard. She also has an inboard diesel which doesn't seem to be too much in the way (it's under the companionway), and fairly good tankage, although the British do tend to skimp in the icebox department. Since ice was never available in the Mediterranean anyway, this didn't seem like much of a problem. They just drank warm drinks and bought fresh food by the day when possible.

By American standards the Tiger is a bit underrigged and is not the liveliest performer in light airs, although the hull is easily driven. In a meltemi, the notorious summer north wind of the Aegean, however, the easily managed rig was a blessing, and the boat could handle quite a blast. A cruising rig that errs on the side of underrigging is usually a better compromise than a large rig.

An option offered by most British builders is that of single or double keel. The latter is a fine feature in British waters, where many harbors are left dry at low tide and boats must sit on "the hard." Ability to remain upright is important, but there is almost nowhere in North America where this feature would be a plus, and it is a slower configuration for sailing, with the added wetted surface and resistance. The single-keel draft is fairly large for a boat of this size and could be a hindrance in some gunkholing areas.

The Tiger's cockpit is far from oversize but better than many British ones, and adequate for four, although with more people aboard it does get a bit squeezy. All in all, though, this is a remarkably big 25-footer.

# The Amphibi-Con

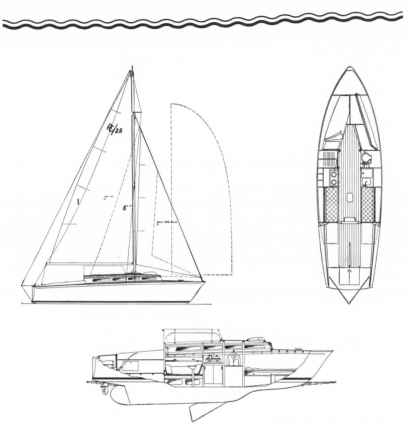

*The 25-foot Amphibi-Con.* 25'5" × 21'8" × 7'9" × 2'4"

Not quite 2 feet longer than the Amphibi-Ette, its bigger sister, the Amphibi-Con had wide acceptance in the prefiberglass era, and for a while had a very active owner's association that was a forerunner of many similar ones that have followed. The members conducted regattas, rendezvous, and winter meetings, where owners exchanged information and experiences profitably and pleasantly. This type of organization has become the accepted thing in many classes of one-design auxiliaries.

71

The main difference between the Amphibi-Con and Amphibi-Ette was that the 2 feet of added length were used to have a separate head compartment between the main cabin and the forward cabin, while the Amphibi-Ette's head was under a filler section in the forward bunk. This is a graphic example of what each extra foot or two of length can mean in added space in a boat.

The Amphibi-Con was completely strip-planked with a round-bilge hull in contrast to the Amphibi-Ette's chine and plywood top-sides, but the Amphibi-Ette hull was basically a bit faster, as the boats sailed fairly evenly despite the Amphibi-Con's greater length and slightly larger sail area.

There were also variations on the convertible hood in different Amphibi-Cons. Some had hard pop-tops instead of a canvas hood, and the hood was really just a cabin top, as it fit over an extension of the cabin trunk and did not make an open cockpit of the main cabin when removed, which was the case with the Amphibi-Ette. Although most had outboard power, a few Amphibi-Cons were fitted with small in-boards.

The popularity of this boat and its success in many regattas did a great deal to promote the idea of trailable auxiliaries.

# The Bianca 27

When we cruised in this well-built and well-appointed Danish sloop in Denmark's Fyn Archipelago in 1971, having been under the rather provincial impression that most advances in the design of stock auxiliaries were of American origin, we were surprised to find that she embodied some nice features that hadn't yet made their way to the States.

Number one was an inboard diesel small enough and light enough to be practical in a boat under 30 feet. It had always been my thought that inboard gas engines were a poor idea in cruising sailboats and that it was better to have an outboard for power in boats under 30 feet. The Bianca, however, had a ten-horsepower Bukh motor, a Danish product that has since become available in other countries, and it was ideal for the job. It started with no fuss every time and puck-pucked along at low rpms very efficiently. Since some of our cruising was amid sand flats cut through by winding channels, we used the motor fairly often and well.

The Bianca was an adaptation of the classic folkboat type, with deep draft for her size, a full-bodied hull, a flat transom with forward rake, and a big barn-door outboard rudder. Her beam was relatively narrow so that accommodations for four were a bit tight, but for two the bunks were comfortable and living was easy. She had other touches we hadn't seen, such as a foot pump for the water taps in the galley. This idea has now spread widely, as it makes good sense in freeing an extra hand for working in the galley, or just holding on if the going is rough, when drawing water.

The deep, full hull with a generous keel made a sea-kindly and able boat, dry in a slop, and a good performer on all points, although naturally giving something away in speed due to the amount of wetted surface. She had the feel of a real little ship, great in areas where draft is not a problem and where open water is expected, but a bit hampered in gunkholing country.

*The Bianca 27.* 27' × 23' × 7'9" × 6'

She was also the first boat we had cruised in that made use of weather cloths around the cockpit and a dodger forward of it, although the windshield at the forward end of the Amphibi-Ette's hood was a form of dodger. Most Scandinavian boats are fitted with cockpit weather cloths since Baltic and North Sea spray is cold, but fortunately we did not have to rely on them in the fair weather we enjoyed.

Although I believe the Bianca has gone out of production, she is an example of a type that remains very popular in Scandinavia and can be seen by the dozens in any cruising harbor in Denmark, Sweden, Norway, and Finland.

# The Compass 29

Designed and built in New Zealand, and used by us on charter in Australia's Whitsunday Islands (their equivalent of bareboating the Virgins), this compact, shippy, and able boat is a perfect example of trying to do too much with the space available, although there is always some justification when a boat is intended for full-time bareboat chartering. In order to make her an attractive bargain for charter parties, she is billed as a sleeping six, and there are, in truth, places for six people to lay their heads. However none of the bunks is quite big enough for a full-grown adult, and six people would be all over each other in trying to go through the functions of daily living. Of course, a family with young children could make do, about the only way to justify the six-sleeper tag.

For a couple, we found her comfortable, although the double bunk forward, since modified and enlarged by the removal of locker shelves, was just not quite big enough, and it was a bit difficult for even two people to move around the cabin freely, as the space between the dinette and galley is narrow. One thing about quarter berths: when only two people are aboard, they make a wonderful place to tuck items like camera cases, empty duffels, and extra blankets out of the way. The cockpit is a good-size one, but movement past the steering wheel was a bit difficult.

A roller-reefing jib is set on an aluminum spar that is actually a boom section for a smaller boat. It works smoothly, and the jib can be reefed as desired and used at that size. This is a roller reefer, not just a roller furler. A reel winch for the main halyard is awkward and invites jams (I have never been partial to this type of winch). A midships traveler makes the main easy to handle, but a hatchless companionway is therefore required and is quite small for adults to negotiate. A handy touch on the main is a line running along the boom with small pieces

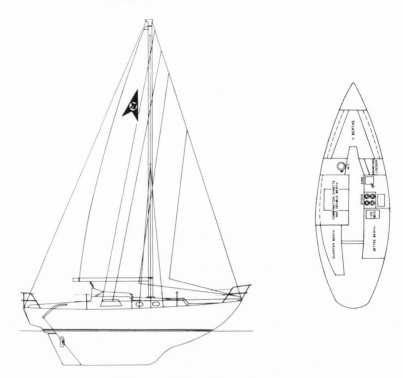

*The Compass 29.* 28'6" × 22'6" × 8' × 4'

of line and shock cord attached to it at intervals for use as furling stops. Each piece of shock cord has a knotted end that goes through a small loop in the end of its companion piece of line, and is held in place by its own tension—quick and handy, but a lot of stuff flapping around when not in use. Jiffy reefing is also very handy, but adds to the considerable collection of line along the boom.

Engine access to the ten-horsepower Yanmar diesel, an adequate plant, is not bad under the companionway, but a bit tight for getting at the machinery. For some reason all engine instruments are below instead of being in the cockpit, which is not very handy when you want to check the oil and water guages or change rpms.

She proved a lively and responsive sailer, dry, stiff, and able, and we had breezes up to 20 knots to test her. Visibility forward is good, and the rig is generally easy to handle.

While we wouldn't want a crowd aboard her, she proved a delight-ful boat for two of us, and it even wasn't too tough to get the anchor up, although she was equipped with an all-chain rode, a necessity in waters where anchoring is often over bottom that is strewn with coral heads. Any kind of line, even the toughest nylon, can chafe through if it wraps around a coral head or the edge of a reef.

Except for where a couple of brand names would show, one could easily imagine that this boat, popular Down Under, was built as a stock boat in the United States.

# The Columbia 29

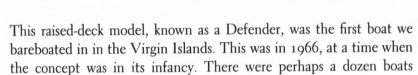

This raised-deck model, known as a Defender, was the first boat we bareboated in in the Virgin Islands. This was in 1966, at a time when the concept was in its infancy. There were perhaps a dozen boats available out of St. Thomas that year, just before the idea of fleet operations caught on, and the Defender was well adapted to the purpose.

We had another couple with us, and the raised-deck construction provided more cabin space than any other 29-footer we have ever been in. There was a big double bunk, convertible from a dinette in the main cabin, and a stateroom forward that was given a measure of privacy by some rather complicated folding doors that worked to shut off the head compartment, between the two cabins, from either of them, depending on who was in it. The galley ran along the entire starboard side of the main cabin as one long counter, the same layout we later had in our OI 36, and it is a good one for in-port use, although sometimes a bit difficult when underway on the starboard tack. The counter configuration makes it easy for more than one person at a time to work there, a pleasant feature when two couples are cruising. A galley that is safe and efficient at sea is usually a one-cook affair.

The space in this boat was enough to make an inboard engine practical, and while I have never felt that a raised deck made for beauty in a boat (it is hard to disguise or camouflage the bulk), I remembered how how roomy this boat was when we were considering buying the CSY 37.

*The Columbia 29.* 28'10" × 22'6" × 9'2" × 4'3"

# The Ranger 29

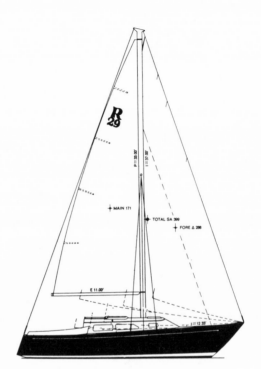

*The Ranger 29.*

We had a cruise in this Gary Mull–designed sloop out of the Costa Smeralda on the Italian island of Sardinia, ranging through the islands in the Strait of Bonifacio to Corsica and back, and she was fine for two of us. Again, though, for purposes of providing maximum bunks in a bareboat, her layout was set up to provide berths for seven. The stateroom forward, which we used, has a double bunk, and the main cabin has a double bunk converted from the dinette, a double quarter berth, and a single settee. Lots of lying-down space here, but imagine seven people revolving around each other in the limited space between bunks.

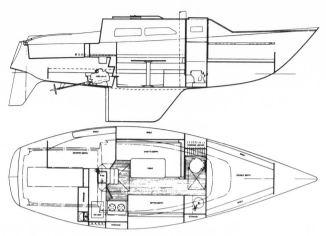

*The Ranger 29.* 28'7" × 23' × 9'4" × 4'5"

Again, we used the quarter berth for stowage, left the dinette in position, and were extremely comfortable.

The boat is an American design, but the ones available for charter in Italy were built there on license, as there is a heavy import tax on foreign-built boats. As far as I could tell, construction standards had been well maintained, and the gear and equipment were all top grade.

This was one of the better sailboats we have cruised in in this size range, a very lively performer on all points, responsive and quick. When we were caught in a rather strong norther, she took the big seas rolling from the open Mediterranean in good style. We had to work our way directly to windward out of a narrow bay cutting deeply into the north coast of Sardinia into the teeth of the norther, and we were able to make good progress despite the steep chop with just a reefed main. (I expected to need a jib, but I thought I'd try it under main alone before messing with the foredeck in those conditions, and she made good progress with just the main so we stuck to it.) This was a good example of why many people like to have a boat with good performance characteristics for cruising. There are some spots in which you really want sailing ability even when the boat is a pure cruiser.

It was good to catch up again with our old friend, the ten-horsepower Bukh diesel, in this boat, and again it proved reliable and just about right for the size of boat.

# The Hinkley Sou'wester Jr.

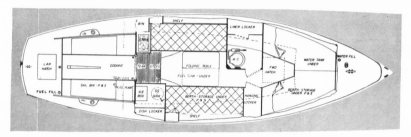

*The 30-foot Hinckley Sou'Wester Jr.* 30'3" × 22' × 8'9" × 4'7"

This design harks back to an earlier day, when it was considered normal to confine the accommodations in a 30-footer to four people. There was a cabin forward with two bunks, a main cabin with two bunks, a table, and a galley, and a head between the two cabins—and that was it. There was no thought of "six-sleepers" or convertible dinettes or double use of space, and this was conventional thinking in cruising boats until the late 1950s or early 1960s. In fact a Hinckley model previous to this one, the Hinckley 21, whose name was based on the waterline length, not her overall length of 29 feet, only had bunks for three people. She had transom berths in the main cabin and one pipe berth forward. We cruised in one with another couple in the early 1950s, and I slept in the cockpit. It was fine except when fog condensed on the boom and dripped on my nose.

The Sou'wester Jr. was originally built in wood and was one of the first designs Hinckley decided to convert to fiberglass. Making sure of the untested new material, they put extra-heavy amounts into this boat, and the result was an extremely strong little yacht, built like a battleship. The extra weight cut down on her overall speed, but she had a good, deep-bodied, sea-kindly hull and was a perfectly good performer for cruising.

*The 30-foot Hinckley Sou'Wester Jr.*

She was also built in the days before diesel was almost universally adapted to cruising auxiliaries, and there was a rather ancient, cranky gas engine in the boat we cruised in in Maine in the early 1970s. I think it was the last boat with an inboard gas engine that I have cruised in, and reminds me that one of the happiest developments in cruising boats has been the general availability of smaller and smaller diesels. I would hate to go back to being shipmates with a gasoline engine now.

In her day the Sou'wester Jr. was a fine cruising boat for two couples or a small family, and I include her here as an example of the way thinking on layouts has progressed under the impact of the increased popularity of cruising auxiliaries, especially in smaller sizes, in recent years.

# The O'Day 32

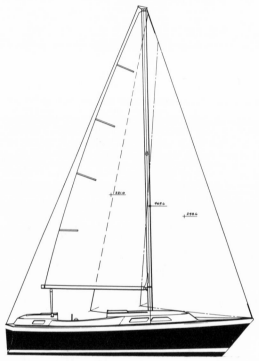

The O'Day 32.

Following my remarks about the Sou'wester Jr. and use of space, here is a boat that makes the absolute most of its overall length, in a practical, sensible way, more than almost any cruising boat I have sailed in. It is also a contrast to the "battleship" construction of the Hinckley from the early days of fiberglass in that this is a much more lightly built boat using considerably different techniques.

With a generous beam and a high freeboard, plus an ingenious

84

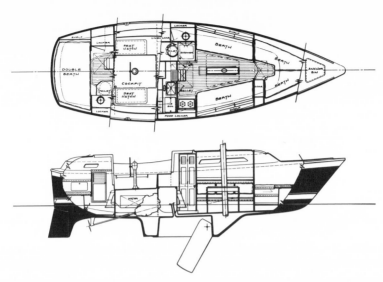

*The O'Day 32.* 31'7" × 27'3" × 10'6" × 7'1"

arrangement of accommodations, this is the smallest boat I have seen that employs a center-cockpit configuration successfully. The after cabin takes up very little fore-and-aft space since the beam is carried well aft, allowing a double bunk to be placed athwartships there. There is also a head right next to the bunk, and a basin, but these cannot be enclosed, of course. The bunk itself is roomy and comfortable, and there is not that "dog kennel" feeling here that some small cabins have.

The cockpit is perfectly adequate for the boat's size, and the main and forward cabins are conventionally laid out in accommodations one would more or less expect in a 32-footer without the plus of the after cabin. The result is a layout that has proved very popular in bareboat chartering, especially for bargain seekers, as there is bunk space for as many people as in much bigger boats, but at a lower price.

As always, there has to be some way of "paying" for all this living space, and this comes from the high freeboard and lightness of construction, which make the boat a bit corky in a slop at sea, but it is not a serious fault in inshore waters, and the compromise comes out quite well.

# The Maxi 9.5

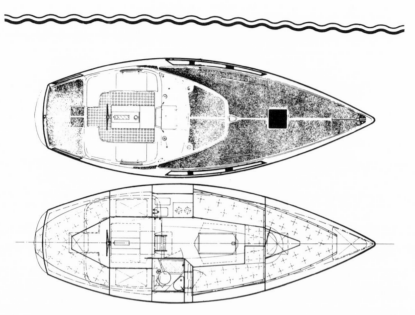

*The Maxi 9.5.* 32′ × 25′9″ × 10′7″ × 4′10″

There are some eight million people in Sweden and about eight hundred thousand of them own boats, mostly small cruising auxiliaries under 35 feet. It is only natural, then, that the Swedes have become experienced in designing and building boats of this type. The Danish Bianca 27, already discussed, is typical of the folkboat type and its near cousins that have been popular all through Scandinavia for many years. This is a classic, traditional model, but there are also some very new, modern designs on Swedish waterways that are being exported to sailing areas all over the world.

One of the most successful designers and sailors in Sweden is Pelle Petterson, who has won fame as an Olympic sailor, Star Class champion, and the man who put Sweden's first America's Cup campaign together in 1977. He was the designer, sailmaker, and skipper of *Sve-*

*The Maxi 9.5.*

*rige.* He is also head of his own boatbuilding company, which produces boats under the trade name of Maxi, and the number after the Maxi name refers to its overall length in meters (9.5 in this case, or 32 feet).

The Maxi boats are very modern looking with contoured hulls, tinted Perspex ports for one-way visibility set into the sheer stripe, and a streamlined-looking raised-deck configuration. The hull is designed for speed and sailing performance is of a high order, but there is plenty of room for accommodations, and these have been well thought out. Perhaps the only complaint Americans might make is a tendency to keep icebox space rather small.

Other than that, there is a small but usable after cabin for just a double bunk that is hardly noticeable in her lines, and a main cabin that can seat up to ten people. The cockpit is also roomy and can handle that many people when entertaining at a rendezvous. And there are nice touches like a stowage bin for the jib at the stem and a section of the after pulpit that converts into a swimming ladder.

I only had a short day sail in Sweden in a Maxi 9.5, but I was impressed with what I saw and with how she sailed.

# The Sandpiper 32

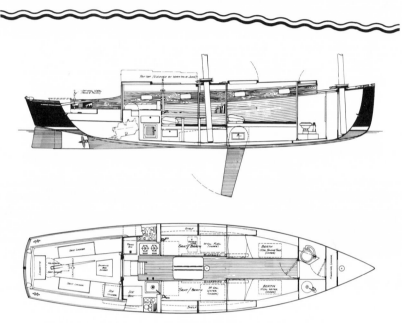

*The Sandpiper 32.* 32'8" × 28'4" × 8' × 1'7"

So many of the boats I have sailed in over the years have been so similar as to have almost come out of the same cookie cutter, but the Sandpiper 32 is very different. The hull is a traditional one, the classic sharpie, which is basically a big flat-bottomed rowboat with refinements. A fined entry, a little deadrise in the hull, and a tapered run aft make this an extremely easily driven hull, with a production price per foot in fiberglass less than two-thirds that of conventional deep-bodied keel boats in the same size range.

Sandpiper, designed by Walter Scott for his own use and then adapted into production, only draws 1 foot 7 inches with her bilge-boards up, which means that she can poke into all sorts of places normally denied cruising auxiliaries, and yet she has been well enough

*The Sandpiper 32.*

thought out so that she provides comfortable cruising quarters for four. A young family, for which this boat would be ideally adapted, could bunk a couple of extra youngsters in the cockpit. (The bilgeboards are housed in the bunk frames, and therefore are not an obstacle in the cabin.)

There is 5 feet of sitting headroom under the cabin trunk, but Scott, who used to own an Amphibi-Con, has adapted a feature of that pioneering design by including a pop-top section over the galley at the after end of the trunk. This can be raised via hand-cranked jacks to give

90

over 6 feet of headroom over the galley, and screens and weather cloths can be added if there is a need for them. The galley is on both sides of the cabin at the after end, with the stove on one side and sink and ice chest on the other. The ice chest has access from both cabin and cockpit, which is a handy extra. There is also a hanging locker aft of the stove.

A Yanmar twelve-horsepower diesel under the companionway is readily accessible, and the hull is so easily driven that it moves along at an effortless 7 knots under power.

Most of these features are unusual, but the really distinctive thing about the Sandpiper 32 is its rig. This is a cat schooner, with equal-height unstayed masts with wishbone booms, an odd-enough rig in itself, but an even rarer feature is that the masts rotate, furling the sails in that manner. All the sail-control lines come back to the cockpit. The sails are unfurled by pulling on a clew outhaul line that leads from the outer end of the boom back along it and then from its forward end down to the deck. In the production boat, there are two drums at the base of the mast, one for furling and one for unfurling, since the prototype, which we sailed, had some difficulties with friction in unfurling without a drum.

I found that it took some experimenting to get the proper balance in the trim of both sails when on the wind in a blow, as she would stall out if the main was too flat and the foresail too slack, but this balance was corrected in production models, and I was able to change the relative trim enough to make her balance. A conventional schooner rig is offered, but in my book the cat schooner rig with rotating masts completes the picture of an unusual boat with a lot of innovative ideas. A boat like this can open up all sorts of new gunkholing opportunities, a wonderful plus in these days of crowded harbors, and that's what she's for, not passaging offshore in rough seas.

# The Mottle 33

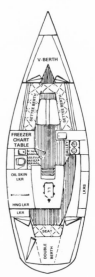

*The Mottle 33.* 32′9½″ × 30′2″ × 10′9″ × 5′3″

The Mottle 33 was also used on charter in Australia's Whitsunday Islands and is representative of a popular type of cruising boat Down Under. She makes good use of her length by including an aft-cabin layout complete with what the Aussies call a "stoop way"—a walk-through without full headroom—and "stoop" is the correct word here. The after cabin has only partial headroom unless the hatch is open, but the bunk is a big one and good use is made of the stoopway for food stowage in covered bins.

The galley set-up is efficient in use of space, although there are a couple of awkward things about it. The sink is a bit small and is placed outboard, so that it is a long stretch to lean over it, made more difficult because the deadrise of the hull curves the sole up at this spot. Also,

*The Mottle 33.*

if you reach for the sink while the stove is on, one elbow is in danger of being singed. The sink and drain board should probably be reversed.

The head location is very central, but not the best for privacy. The shower head also serves as the water tap for the sink, worked by a foot pedal, saving on hardware installation. There is no hot water system provided for. The settee berths and forward double are of fairly small proportions, and six people would not be comfortable in this layout, although it would do for a family with children.

Sailing qualities are satisfactory for cruising, and the rig is easily managed, although, as I have said, I personally do not like reel winches, which seem to be popular for halyards in Australia. Jiffy reefing is an excellent addition. The cockpit is comfortable for sailing, if not overly large. The companionway arrangement, with the ladder set back in to the cockpit so that no sliding hatch is needed, allows a midships traveler for the main sheet, otherwise difficult to do in a center-cockpit boat. The companionway ladder is steep and the opening is a bit small, especially for a 6-footer in foul-weather gear. The cockpit could be rigged for a Bimini. For some reason there didn't seem to be any cockpit scuppers.

Because of Australian regulations on safety for charter boats, the engine compartment is completely enclosed for fire protection, and access to the diesel is quite difficult. The Mottle has the same placement for engine instruments that the Compass does—in the cabin below—which is a minor annoyance.

All in all, this boat is a generally successful use of 33 feet for cruising.

# The Bristol 33

We cruised in the Halsey Herreshoff–designed Bristol 33 in the era when boats were supposed to race and cruise well in a dual-purpose role. This was in the late 1960s, and it was not too long after that that the two types went off on wide splits, the skinned-out IOR Grand Prix boats representing one direction and the all-out cruising boats the other.

In the era when a boat could do both, the Bristol 33 was an excellent compromise, and she would still make a good cruising boat that could do well in club racing and local overnight races. Halsey is the third generation of the famous Bristol, Rhode Island, family of naval architects. Nathanael Herreshoff, the "Wizard of Bristol," was his grandfather, famous for his America's Cup defenders from 1893 to 1920, and the single most influential designer and innovator in the history of American yachting. Halsey's father was A. Sidney deW. Herreshoff, and his uncle was L. Francis Herreshoff, both active and successful designers in their own right. The best known yacht from the second generation is *Ticonderoga,* designed by L. Francis.

The Bristol 33, which we took for a week's cruise in southern New England, featured the "Herreshoff bow" which Halsey carried on from the designs of his grandfather. This is a gracefully raked bow with virtually a straight line from stem to waterline, and distinctively hollowed sections in the flare. It makes for fine windward ability, with a dry and easy motion, and while others have used the same principle, it is still very much a Herreshoff trademark. The boat had a big cockpit and long cabin trunk carried well forward, which made for full headroom for the entire length of the cabin. She had a convertible dinette and the galley right at the main hatch, and there was maximum bunk space for seven in an amazingly roomy cabin. The cockpit was carried all the way aft to the transom, but we found there was a weakness in

*The Bristol 33.* 33'4" × 26'6" 10'3" × 5'7"

this—water on deck would eventually gutter into it, making it a sudden sitz bath.

This was one of the few faults in a well-planned boat, but the only other obvious one was rather serious to the cruising sailor. She had a separate spade rudder, and it had to be carefully tended every instant when under sail and power or she would spin out in a 180° flip. You couldn't so much as glimpse at the chart or pick up the binoculars with a moment's inattention or the boat would go into a complete spin. I mentioned this in an article published at the time, and the next year at the boat show in New York the builder took me beneath a new model of the boat and showed me that the rudder was now attached to a skeg. He told me how much the tooling to make this change had cost, and said, with some asperity, that it was known as the "Bill Robinson memorial skeg."

Somewhat abashed, I nevertheless still cling to my belief that a boat should get in a groove and almost steer herself, especially for comfortable cruising.

# The Comfort 34

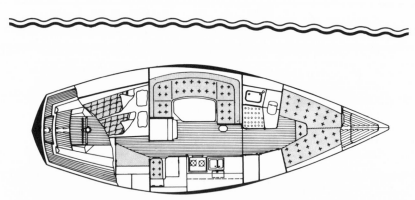

*The Comfort 34.* 33'6" × 28'8" × 11'5" × 6'

Construction of this boat came about in an unusual way. Her builder, a young Swede named Sven Enoch of Steningsund, twenty-four miles north of Gothenburg on the west coast of Sweden, was in the aluminum business, with no background in boatbuilding, when he was selected to build the Swedish challenger for the America's Cup, the 12-meter *Sverige,* which was launched in 1976. Enoch was chosen for the job because of his expertise in aluminum welding, and in the process of building *Sverige* he became so fascinated with boats that he started his own company, Sweden Boats, and continued to build yachts in aluminum and fiberglass.

His first stock design was the Comfort 34, designed by Kenneth Albinsson and Jens Ostman, available either as a cruising boat or in a cruiser/racer version, and the result is a beautifully built and appointed modern boat that has a very comfortable and roomy layout for her size, and performs well enough to have taken some prizes in Swedish racing. She is a luxury boat at the top of the price scale, and she shows it in her appointments and in such touches as a nicely laid teak deck.

I cruised in one for a week in the skerries of Sweden's west coast, and she proved a very able and lively performer, responsive, stiff, and

*The Comfort 34.*

close-winded, dry and comfortable when the going became a bit sloppy, and easily driven in light air. Her layout is long on room at the expense of privacy, with a large double bunk under the forward end of the cockpit, giving on a good-size main cabin with a dinette and transom bunk. A head compartment and private cabin are forward. Extra space was gained through the use of a twenty-three-horsepower Volvo sail-drive diesel, a through-hull installation that doesn't take much room. It is located under the companionway steps, with the drive going vertically through the hull to a folding propeller. The space that would normally be taken up by transmission and propeller shaft could be given over to the big double bunk, and there is also room for a sail-stowage

99

*The Comfort 34.*

bin next to the bunk. She handled well under power with speed of about 6 knots.

On deck, she is clean and uncluttered and easy to handle, and everything about her bespeaks quality.

# The OI 36

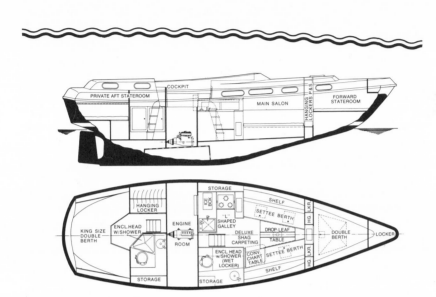

*The Morgan Out Island 36.* 35′10″ × 28′ × 11′ × 3′9″

The Morgan Out Island 36 was developed from the mold of a Morgan 38 that was designed as an ocean racer under the Cruising Club of America Rule. When that was replaced by the International Offshore Rule in the late 1960s, use was made of the now-outmoded ocean-racing mold by adapting an Out Island layout to the 38-foot hull. The result was a cruising boat that sailed remarkably well in comparison to most boats with the same number of accommodations. The OI 36 failed to achieve wide popularity, however, because the main cabin was not quite roomy enough to appeal to motorboat owners who were switching to sail. They wanted saloon-like space and had no idea about sailing qualities, and this was the market the OI line had to appeal to. After the OI 36 went out of production, enough people had learned of its special qualities to make it a sought-after used boat.

We owned the OI 36 *Tanagra* for five years and were very pleased with her on almost all counts. We chose her for the same reasons that

*The Morgan Out Island 36.*

led us to the CSY 37—size range, two private cabins with separate heads, shallow draft, and sailing ability. We cruised in her from Cape Cod to the Exumas over several seasons and found her livable and able. We did agree that the main cabin was small, as was the forward stateroom, and the cockpit could also have been a bit roomier, but the after cabin was very roomy and comfortable. On the few occasions when we cruised with six people, conditions were quite crowded and it is always inconvenient and awkward at breakfast time to reconvert the dinette from night duty as a bunk.

In an attempt to overcome adverse reactions to the dinette version of the main cabin, Morgan came out with a layout that put the galley to port and the head to starboard immediately forward of the cockpit. The main cabin was forward of this and had good room at a drop-leaf table for meals and entertaining, but the settees were too narrow to be real bunks, and the "forward cabin" was just an undersize double bunk in the peak, with crawl-in access. This layout was fine for in-port entertaining, but no good for sleeping anyone but kids or midgets, except in the after cabin, which was unchanged from the original layout.

Despite its shortcomings, the original OI 36 layout provided a great deal of accommodation space in 36 feet, and the boat had good performance qualities under sail and power. She made about 7.2 knots using just under one gallon of diesel fuel per hour with a Perkins 4-108 engine. With 60 gallons of fuel and 175 of water, she had a better than average cruising range of more than four hundred miles under power. The main water supply of 100 gallons of pressurized water was supplemented by a 75-gallon tank under the forward bunk that was on hand pumping only, so there was good backup should the pressure water system fail.

Entrance to the engine room was awkward, but the space itself was quite large, and once you had made it through the small door, most of the equipment was reasonably accessible.

The rig was easily handled, and the roller-furling jib was especially handy. It was set up on its own luff wire, there was a separate headstay on which other jibs could be hanked, and the roller furler could be lowered on deck if there was any problem in getting it completely furled or some other form of jam. The high boom allowed sailing with the Bimini up.

The OI 36 deserved to be more popular than it was—it was popular with me.

# The Excalibur 36

In 1968, we chartered a 36-foot sloop of this class out of Grenada in the earliest days of bareboating in that area, and I include her here as an example of the kind of boat that was popular then and representative of general thinking as a racer/cruiser. She was designed by a Dutchman, van de Stadt, and built of fiberglass in England, and looking back on her it is amazing to remember how very small she was in comparison to the 36- and 37-foot boats we are now used to. In cubic footage she was perhaps half as big as our own CSY 37 of 1978 vintage, and while she might have been a bit livelier as a sailboat, she did not have an outstanding edge in that department, and she was quite wet in a seaway.

Her accommodations were basically for four and they just about made that, as she was very compact in all respects. They were perfectly all right, but there was one terrible problem in trying to get back and forth from cabin to cockpit. Instead of a sliding hatch, she had an oval opening with a slight contoured bulge above it in the cabin trunk (or coach roof, as the British would have it), and for moderately awkward middle-aged Americans of average or slightly larger than average size, it was a real acrobatic performance to negotiate it. We had one 6-foot 2-inch, two-hundred-pounder with us, and he confined himself to one trip up in the morning and another back at night, refusing to scrunch through the thing any more often than that. This is a memory that sticks in my mind.

While a spade rudder and fin keel made her a bit skittish in the steering, she did provide us with some good sailing, and she was definitely easy to handle. I gather she won quite a few races in her time.

*The Excalibur 36.* 36′ × 26′ × 9′6″ × 6′

# The Pearson Pilothouse 36

*The Pearson Pilothouse 36.*

A growing trend going into the 1980s has been to add more and more powerboat comforts to cruising sailboats while maintaining basic sailing ability, and one manifestation of this trend has been to add pilot houses or motor-sailer-type deckhouses to boats in the middle size ranges. It used to be that a deckhouse was looked on as ungainly and a complete concession to motor-sailerdom in anything below 55 feet or so, but that is no longer the case.

A good example is the Pearson Pilothouse 36 sloop, introduced for

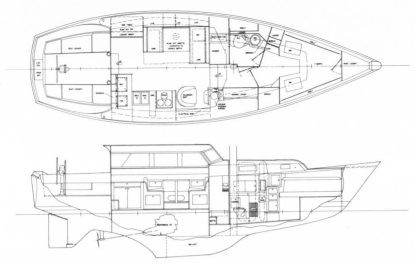

*The Pearson Pilothouse 36.* 36'5" × 30' × 11'5½" × 4'6"

the 1979–80 season, with a well-thought-out application of a deckhouse or pilot house on the already fully established hull used for the 365 cruising auxiliary. Bill Shaw, Pearson's chief designer and general manager, has long had a reputation for attention to the little details that make a difference in a boat's livability, and he has put this ability to use here.

In an afternoon sail in a typical sea breeze southerly on Narragansett Bay, I was able to determine that this boat acts like a true sailboat, as we tacked down the bay in company with several other boats in the same size range, and the layout has been carefully worked out to provide motor-sailer-type comfort. A key element in this is an inside helmsman's station to starboard in the pilot house. For a retired couple making their way down the Intracoastal Waterway in the fall, this would be just the thing for raw days that rush the season, and the pilot house also provides a large living and entertaining area, with a galley to starboard and settee to port. This can serve as a berth when guests are aboard, but the basic idea is a comfortable boat for two, with all the amenities needed for living aboard for long periods of time. The head and stowage spaces are particularly roomy, carrying out the theme even further, there is a generator to take care of all the electrical goodies

*The Pearson Pilothouse 36.*

that make living aboard more pleasant, and a forty-horsepower Wester-beke diesel gives maximum power performance for the waterline length of 30 feet.

This boat is an excellent example of specialization that fits a specific need, in this case in what seems to be a growing trend.

# The Carter 37

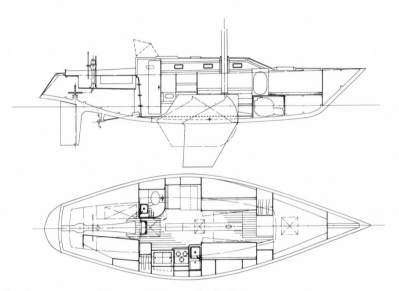

*The Carter 37.* 37′8″ × 29′6″ × 11′10″ 7′

Although I have spent a lot of time and space pointing out that the requirements of cruising and ocean-racing boats have become impossible to reconcile in one boat, there are owners who want to do both and there are designers willing to take on the challenge. Obviously, racing considerations have to come first, and it then becomes a question of how to adapt some cruising amenities to a boat that will stand up to modern IOR competition, where weight has become such a factor.

Dick Carter, long an innovator in ocean-racing designs, produced this custom, one-off plan in which the method of construction takes care of the weight problem, and convertibility below decks solves the question of cruising amenities. Naturally, such cruising features as bow-chock anchors, propane tanks in the cockpit, voluminous tankage, and roller-furling sails would not be part of the picture.

She is of cold-molded four-ply construction. The inner three layers are diagonal, and the outer one is fore-and-aft. Each layer is 3.5 millimeters thick, for a total of 14 millimeters, or just over half an inch. The inner ply is African mahogany, the middle two are yellow pine, and the fore-and-aft layer is Honduras mahogany. In addition to saving weight, this construction method is a space saver in that the laminated frames can be widely spaced, but it is so light that reinforcement is necessary. Carbon-fiber threads are used as reinforcement between the first and second and third and fourth layers of ply, wrapped around the hull.

The weight saving this provides is transmitted into decent living accommodations for four people to cruise in, but the layout can also be adapted for racing. The large double bunk, which serves as an owner's cabin in cruising, becomes sail stowage, and the transom bunks in the main cabin are hot-bunked by a racing crew. The head is enclosed, and the galley is a full one for cruising comfort.

A special feature of the boat is a retractable keel (not a centerboard) that can be hydraulically controlled for operations in shallow water, although she races with the keel fixed in place and a fairing plate filling the slot around it to reduce turbulence, assuring a better rating than a boat with a movable keel or board.

The keel weldment of stainless steel and the lead keel itself both serve as ballast, and engine placement also helps in weight distribution. The Perkins 4-108 diesel is located in a box between the forward bunk and the mast, and power is transmitted by a Volvo pump and hydraulic drive unit via two hoses that are led aft along the keel case.

A sophisticated boat like this takes getting used to, and there were bugs in her construction and engineering that took some working out in the beginning, but she has done well racing, and she is a perfectly pleasant cruising boat for four when off duty from the racing circuit.

# The CSY 37

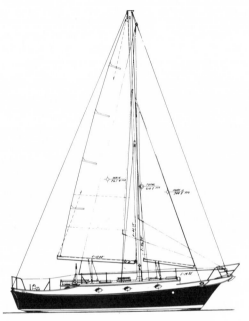

*The CSY 37.* 37′3″ × 29′2′ × 12′ × 4′9″

There has already been considerable discussion of this boat in Part I on "Choosing a Boat," since she ended up as our choice for the latest Robinson family yacht. To avoid repetition, I merely point out, with the layout plan in view, how the tricabin set-up has been ingeniously worked out, with the very real help of the raised-deck feature. I have never been partial to this from an esthetic point of view, but it is a wonderful practical feature. In handling it, I would have liked the forward corners of the raised deck, at the break above the foredeck, to be contoured rather than sticking out as a sharp protrusion. They stick out farther than any other spot on the boat and have a proclivity for encountering pilings in landings that are not perfectly executed.

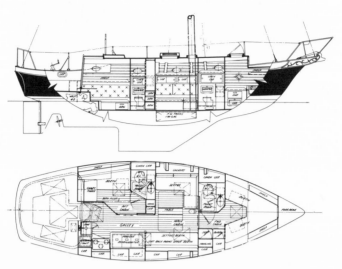

*The CSY 37.*

Also, the step down from the raised deck on each side of its after end tends to be a water catcher when on the windward side in rough going, since the scupper is on the outboard side. This doesn't happen very often.

Below, no one cabin is very big, so there is no great sense of space anywhere below decks (in contrast to the other version of the boat that has a big main cabin), but I still prefer this layout for our use. The great number of hatches (six) is a real plus in the tropics. We are glad we chose the shallow-draft model as we haven't noticed any problem with sailing ability, and the less draft the better when poking through areas like the Florida Keys and the Bahamas.

One addition to the sail plan that I ordered belatedly (and am glad I did) was a Flasher, the poleless cruising spinnaker developed by Charles Ulmer and since adapted in their own version by other sailmakers. This has worked very well and has added real zip to downwind performance. It will not stay full dead before the wind, but is effective from a broad-off, quartering reach to a point where the apparent wind is just forward of the beam. It is rigged like a drifter, with the tack attached at the bowplate and a collar holding the tack pennant close to the forestay. It's a relatively light sail, not intended for winds above

*The CSY 37.*

12–14 knots, but it is a good solution to those downwind blues many cruising boats suffer from. On *Tanagra* we had a pole for winging out the jib, and while it worked pretty well it was a nuisance to rig and had a narrow range of effectiveness.

A design feature that contributes to added living space is a V-drive for the Westerbeke 4-108 diesel through a Warner two-to-one reduction gear. I have found engine access very good through a big cockpit hatch and through the companionway stairs, which slide back from the opening. As designed, there was no insulation for sound in the engine compartment, which made for a high noise level, especially with the Bimini top rigged, but material was added, greatly reducing the problem. A removable dodger that snaps onto the front of the Bimini has been a great help in one or two rough passages, but it hampers movement forward out of the cockpit. As I said before, it's always a case of compromise, but the ones made here have worked out well for us.

# The O'Day 37

*The O'Day 37. 37′ × 30′4″ × 11′2″ × 5′*

The O'Day Company started by building small one-designs and day sailers, gradually increasing the size of the top of its line as owners wanted to move up to a bigger boat while maintaining brand loyalty, and the introduction of this center-cockpit sloop in 1978 marked a big step up. John Deknatel, who has been responsible for most of the recent O'Day designs, put together one of the best looking, best proportioned boats in this size range, a boat that sails extremely well for one with full cruising accommodations.

In a Virgin Islands charter cruise, we found her fast and maneuverable, reacting particularly well to the sudden puffs that often sweep

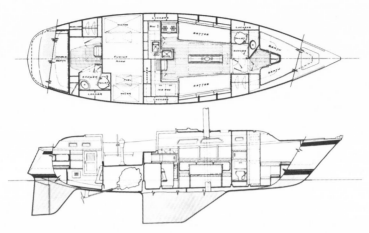

*The O'Day 37.*

down in the lee of island hills. Instead of laying over and wallowing at the onset of a puff, she would stand up to it and accelerate quickly, feeling like a real performer.

It was interesting to me that the design does not include a walk-through, as this contributes greatly to the relatively low profile of the boat and the lack of awkward bulk that makes some aft-cabin boats resemble an old Fall River Line steamer. The cockpit is much roomier, and access to the forty-horsepower diesel under the cockpit is therefore much better. Along with the pleasant lines of the hull, the cabins are nicely contoured for a well-proportioned whole. The deck is very clean and easy to move around on, and the rig is simple and efficient.

I was interested in features of the layout, one good and one not so good (that has since been changed). There is no dinette in the main cabin. Rather, two settee berths have a drop-leaf table between them, and to my mind anything that avoids converting a dinette into a bunk is a plus. The galley, spread across the after end of the cabin on both sides of the companionway, has a lot of good working space, but the cook can be safely wedged in near the stove if forced to operate in rough weather.

My only complaint with the boat we had, which was one of the first production boats out, was with the after cabin. It looked fine on paper, with a double berth to port sticking well out into the center of

*The O'Day 37.*

the cabin, and a small seat next to it to starboard, but in practice it didn't work so well. There was no headboard or bulkhead at the head of the bunk, and there was a considerable feeling of insecurity sleeping out in the open like that, with pillows constantly slipping out onto the cabin sole during a restless night. Also, the little seat soon ended up as a handy catchall and would seldom be clear enough to use as a seat.

From this experience, the builders decided to convert to a more conventional thwartships arrangement for the bunk, amid considerable ribbing about the retooling costs I had engendered, so the "Bill Robinson memorial bunk" joined the "memorial skeg" on the Bristol 33 as my minor contributions to cruising yacht design.

O'Day has always admittedly built to a price, with relatively light construction, emphasizing good performance and comfort in coastwise cruising waters, and this very competitively priced boat is a successful example.

# The Heritage 38

*The Heritage 38.* 38′ × 32′ × 12′ × 4′

This is an interesting example of how a boat can be adapted to the special bareboat charter trade. It was designed for private use, but Tortola Yacht Charters, which operates in the British Virgins, ordered a fleet for bareboat operations, and based on the vast experience gained from dealing with thousands of charterers and learning what works and what doesn't work, made a great number of changes in the boats it ordered.

These changes were all designed to add space, convenience, and livability, and there were very few areas of the layout that remained untouched. In the forward cabin the bunks were considered too short, so the head compartment, just aft of this stateroom, was changed from an enclosed head on one side opposite a hanging locker to one compartment the width of the vessel. This provided the same amount of room in less fore-and-aft space so that the forward bunks could be longer.

In the main cabin, the settees were recessed all the way to the skin of the vessel to give more room, and by adding a filler piece across the door to the forward head, nine people can be seated in a comfortable rectangle. In the galley, the lockers behind the sink and stove were made slightly smaller to provide more working space without sacrificing their function, and the positions of stove and sink were switched so that the sink is by the ladder and no one has to reach across the stove to

117

*The Heritage 38.*

get at other areas, like the icebox. This was a feature noted in the Mottle 33, where a switch of positions would have been beneficial.

As stated, I am not strong on walk-throughs to the after cabin, but the Heritage 38 has made good use of the one it has. First of all, there is a wet bar on the port side at the entrance to it, and this is a pleasant touch in a cruising boat, especially a charter boat where every night tends to be party night. The bartender can operate independent of the galley and doesn't have to reach around the cooks and tip over the salad dressing while performing his functions, as long as he remembers to get an ice bucket filled ahead of time.

When we were in the Heritage 38, there was a wicked booby trap at the entrance to the walk-through in the form of a projection sticking down into the space at about forehead height for an adult. It was actually the inside of the corner of the cockpit mold, and constituted a lethal hazard for the short of memory, but I understand this was corrected in later models. The space in the walk-through was well used for food and beverage stowage in specially fitted lockers, plus extra tankage and an access panel to the Perkins 4-1-8 diesel. The only trouble here was some difficulty in getting at the far side of the engine, another disadvantage of walk-throughs in my book.

Some other items I liked were an extension from the shower in the after head that could be used as a deck shower after swimming, and a swimming ladder on the transom that also doubled as a stand for a hibachi.

Under sail, the Heritage 38 was a bit sluggish in light airs, which are unusual in the Virgin Islands (although we had them in a November cruise), but she perked up when the wind blew harder.

# The Hughes 38

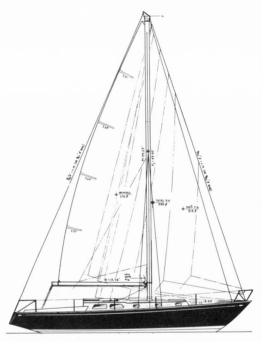

*The Hughes 38.* 37'6" × 28'10" × 10'6" × 6"

This Sparkman & Stephens design had a dual personality. In some way it was made available to two builders, the Canadian company building Hughes boats and Hinckley in Maine, and it was interesting for me, in sailing both models, to see how differently the same hull design can be worked out. The basic hull was the type that was very popular in the late 1960s, a moderate fin keel with skeg rudder, and it did well in ocean races. Hughes built the boat lightly and kept the accommodations fairly simple, so that its boat was very fast and lively, while Hinckley did its traditional job of building very heavily, with extra

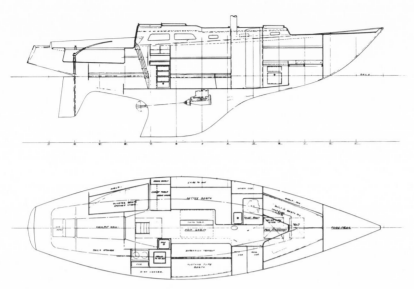

*The Hughes 38.*

thicknesses of fiberglass, and added luxurious cruising accommodations with heavy cabinetry and floorboards, and all the electronic extras. The result was that this boat had a very solid, sturdy feel, handled seas beautifully, and grooved like a locomotive, but was sluggish in light air and had been completely removed from contention in the type of cruiser/racer competition that was then popular.

We had the Hughes on charter in the Grenadines, and a slog past notorious Kick 'em Jenny between Grenada and Carriacou was wet, tough work, with everything damp down below and a feeling of having been in a scrimmage with the Dallas Cowboys, but she had the windward ability to get there, while heavier, full-cruising boats near us took much longer to slug it out in the steep chop, making leeway fast while we clawed into it. I have never been in an S & S hull that did not have good windward ability, and it showed here.

The layout with a stateroom forward, dinette to port, and galley to starboard would have been fine for four, but crowded for six (she was advertised as a six-sleeper), and two of us naturally had all the room in the world. Stowage was adequate for four, but not for more than that.

One trick we used fairly often in this boat was to anchor by the stern, as she would charge around her short keel like an anxious puppy when anchored by the bow, but settled down nicely to a stern anchor. Air circulation was also better with the breeze coming through the main companionway.

It is interesting that in ten years this type of boat has almost disappeared from the bareboating scene, giving way to boats that have much more accommodation room, a less sensitive hull, and almost if not quite the same sailing ability.

# The Pearson 390

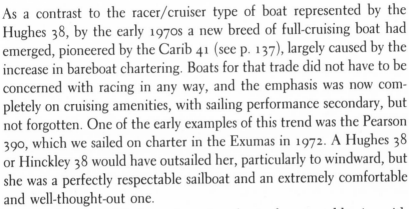

As a contrast to the racer/cruiser type of boat represented by the Hughes 38, by the early 1970s a new breed of full-cruising boat had emerged, pioneered by the Carib 41 (see p. 137), largely caused by the increase in bareboat chartering. Boats for that trade did not have to be concerned with racing in any way, and the emphasis was now completely on cruising amenities, with sailing performance secondary, but not forgotten. One of the early examples of this trend was the Pearson 390, which we sailed on charter in the Exumas in 1972. A Hughes 38 or Hinckley 38 would have outsailed her, particularly to windward, but she was a perfectly respectable sailboat and an extremely comfortable and well-thought-out one.

At the time, I had not been in a boat of comparable size with anywhere near the amount of room provided by her triple-cabin, center-cockpit layout. She had amazing headroom, which gave her a bulky look that designer Bill Shaw tried to break up with a two-tone color scheme and matching angles between the rake of the bow and the break from the raised-deck section, with partial success. With private staterooms and heads forward and aft, and a dinette-to-port, galley-to-starboard layout in the main cabin, she followed what has become almost a standard arrangement in charter boats of this size, and popular with private owners too. The rig was also easy to handle, my first exposure to a roller-furling jib (which sold me immediately), and a moderate-size main that she was beamy and stable enough to carry through breezes up to 30 knots.

A draft of 4 feet 3 inches made her flexible in the shallow waters of the Exumas, and she also had a board for added performance to windward, a practice that has since gone out of style in most full-cruising boats.

Great emphasis was placed on size of icebox and fuel and water

*The Pearson 390.* 39' × 33'8" × 13' × 4'3"

capacity, aimed at lasting through a two-week charter, and the engine was diesel. An added touch that was great fun was a glass window in the hull in the after cabin, a great way to "snorkel" without getting wet, but it was also a bit scary, as it tended to magnify the scene below and make it look as though the bottom were only inches away.

There have been very few changes in the basic concept of aft-cabin, full-cruising boats since the Pearson 390 was introduced, except for the walk-through concept, which, as I've said before, I don't consider an advance.

# The Cal 39

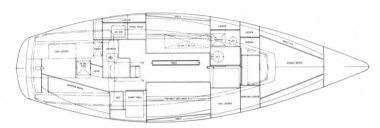

*The Cal 39, alternate layout.*

Two layout versions of this Bill Lapworth–designed classic show two
different modes of thinking on cruising boats, but both of them are on
a hull that combines excellent sailing ability with enough room for real
comfort. Fast enough to be a successful cruiser/racer in competition
below the Grand Prix level, she is about as good a performer as we have
cruised in. Even when relaxing in Virgin Islands sunshine, there is a
certain satisfaction in outsailing everything else in sight—and that we
did very convincingly in the Cal 39.

We were in a boat with a tricabin layout especially arranged for
the bareboat charter trade, where two private cabins and two heads are
deemed a necessary amenity (and rightly so) in boats in this size range.
In this arrangement there is the usual forward stateroom with head,
both very roomy here, a main cabin with dinette to port and a transom
bunk to starboard, the galley aft to starboard, right at the companionway, and a separate enclosed stateroom and head to port. In our boat,
an early version of this layout, the after cabin was not big enough for
a double bunk, which was fine with us since one daughter was our only
crew, but this was altered in later boats to provide room for a double.

The alternate layout, better suited to racing, has just the one head
forward, the galley aft of the dinette on the port side, and a big open

*The Cal 39.* 39' × 32'1" × 12' × 6'8"

quarter berth aft of a navigation station to starboard. As I have stated, navigation stations are a waste of space in charter boats but a help in racing, and this layout would be fine for short overnight or weekend races, and for entertaining a lot of people afterward. I went aboard a boat with this layout in port and had a sense that there was almost too much open space in the cabin, not only for lack of privacy, but also as a possible safety hazard in rough weather, where it is good to have a handhold nearby at all times when moving about.

On deck the Cal 39 is beautifully uncluttered and functional, with a roomy, comfortable cockpit well set up for handling sheets without poking elbows in the helmsman's ribs. A swimming ladder that drops out of the after pulpit is a good and necessary touch for convenience and for safety in a possible man overboard.

Another idea in the Cal 39 that makes sense, but isn't seen in too many boats, is a separation of batteries, one for lights and one for engine starting. In this way, injudicious use of electricity overnight doesn't mean a dead engine in the morning.

# The Concordia 39

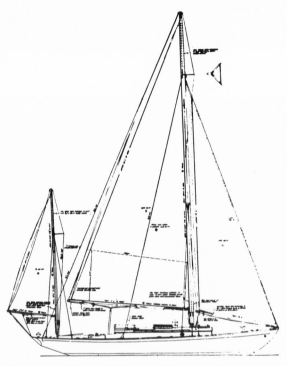

*The Concordia 39.* 39'8" × 29'6" × 10' × 5'11"

As I mentioned in Part I, "Choosing a Boat," this now-ancient design is probably the sweetest, most sea-kindly hull I have ever sailed in, which is a matter of very small degree over some of the excellent boats being described, but that memory stays with me from an experience in the 1950s, and I have watched Concordias and Concordia owners since then and I still feel the same way. Ray Hunt, a relatively untutored genius, as many naval architects are, came up with this design in 1938 as his first assignment, ordered by New England boatbuilder

*The Concordia 39.*

Waldo Howland. It was an immediate success, and it has remained successful for over forty years. The Concordia *Malay* won the 1954 Bermuda Race, and Concordias finished first and second in the MHS Division of the 1978 Bermuda Race, while many more are still providing delightful cruising for owners who refuse to trade them in.

There is no magic to the magic of the Concordia hull. It is simply a very fine-lined, easy hull, with long tapered ends, a rather narrow beam, and a relatively deep draft of 5 feet 11 inches in a well-propor-

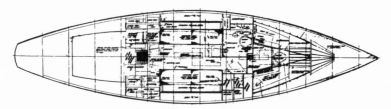

*The Concordia 39.*

tioned keel. It is just a hull that fits the water beautifully and gives a real sense of control and response to the helmsman. It is a hull capable of carrying sail in a heavy breeze, yet easily driven in light stuff, and it also happens to be one of the prettiest hulls still around, with graceful sheer and long, finely contoured ends.

As a modern cruising hull, it does give something away in accommodation space. With her lack of beam and long overhangs in tapered ends, the Concordia has relatively little cabin space for a 39-footer, and there are many boats under 35 feet on the market today that have more space below than the conventional Concordia layout, but she is easy to handle, and four people can be very happy cruising in her.

# The Bermuda 40

*The Hinckley Bermuda 40.* 40'9" × 27'10" × 11'9" × 4'1"

This boat is one of the phenomenal success stories in the cruising auxiliary field. Designed by Bill Tripp and introduced in the late 1950s, it is still being built and is perhaps the "longest running" stock design extant. It isn't the roomiest or fastest 40-footer by any stretch of the imagination, and it is undoubtedly the most expensive, but it has qualities that have made it an enduring favorite, much in demand as a new or used boat.

Paradoxically, expense has something to do with its popularity. As with all Hinckley boats, its reputation for being well and heavily built is deserved, and there is never any skimping in quality from basic construction right on through to the smallest fittings. Hinckley, in fact, makes its own cleats, chocks, rod lugs, and the like, and construction features fiberglass stem and longitudinal stiffeners, and reinforced stress areas. Thick cabin soles of holly inlaid with teak, as well as being handsomely decorative, are a visible example of Hinckley construction standards.

Another attraction for the demanding owner is the attention Hinckley pays to electronic extras, and almost all of them come with a full complement in this field. Buying a Hinckley without them is like ordering a Cadillac without a heater or a radio.

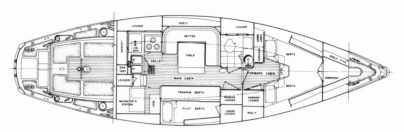

*The Hinckley Bermuda 40.*

When the Bermuda 40 was first introduced, it rated as a threat in offshore racing and turned in performances like a win in the Halifax Race and second overall in the 1963 Transpac, but the switch to IOR in the late 1960s, and the emphasis on light, skinned-out racing machines, soon dimmed this facet of the Bermuda 40's appeal. The broad, rather shallow hull is fairly fast off the wind, especially in a breeze (witness the Transpac performance), and Bermuda 40s did well as a group in the rough going of the 1979 cruising race to Bermuda, which was sailed for the most part on a very close reach. They do not, however, have outstanding windward ability.

The layout is comfortable if no attempt is made to accommodate more than four. Options have been offered over the years in the layout, but in general the emphasis is more on comfort and luxury on a small scale than on roominess. One limiting factor in the sense of space below in a Bermuda 40 is the comparative narrowness of the trunk cabin, but this does have the reverse advantage—once again a compromise—of a clean, uncluttered deck layout, easy to move about on.

The boat has been built as a sloop and a yawl, and a taller rig was offered when the IOR first came in that did add to her speed potential, although not enough to keep up with the racing machines. With her racing career over, however, this boat has hung on as a sturdy, able luxury yacht that has instilled great pride of ownership in those who continue to command her.

*The Hinckley Bermuda 40.*

# The Freedom 40

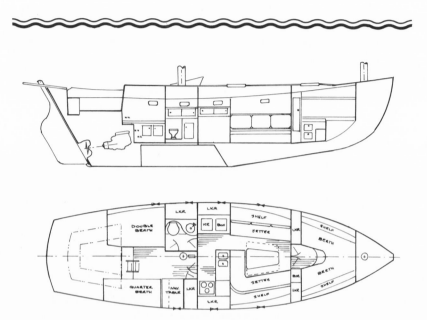

*The Freedom 40. 40' × 35' × 12' × 3'4"*

Of all the boats I have cruised in and written up, none has attracted more reaction and attention than this distinctly individualistic maverick design, called a cat ketch. Gary Hoyt, an American racing sailor living in Puerto Rico and operating in the Virgins, conceived the radical idea for unstayed masts, partly from his experiences sailing a Finn dinghy, which also has an unstayed mast, and commissioned Halsey Herreshoff to design the hull for him. To dramatize her ease of handling, Hoyt refused to install a motor, and it made for an interesting week's cruise in the British Virgin Islands for us to operate completely under sail (with the help at one point in a becalmed harbor of sweep oars to make the last 100 feet to a mooring). Not only was it necessary to make a careful approach to a night's anchorage, but we also had to plan ahead on how to get out of a place. With the constant,

*The Freedom 40.*

reliable winds of the British Virgins and the great number of harbors close together, there was never much worry about making a harbor by nightfall, however.

While Walter Scott calls the Sandpiper 32 rig a cat-schooner with masts of equal height, Hoyt prefers the cat-ketch tag for the Freedom 40, whose masts are also equal, and he calls the sails foresail and mizzen. To reduce sail, he drops the mizzen first, and if it really blows, a staysail can be set between the masts. The Freedom 40 is now in production, and the production boat is equipped with reefing systems on the two sails, as well as an engine, as very few areas are as forgiving for operations under pure sail as the BVI.

The sails are of unusual two-ply construction, wrapping around the masts (which do not rotate like the Sandpiper's), and are joined at the leech by Velcro. This gives better air flow around the wide-sectioned masts. Raising and lowering them is akin to handling a gaff sail, as the forward end of the wishbone boom must be elevated at the same time the sail is being hoisted, so two halyards must be worked. The wishbone acts like a vang, as its angle holds the clew down and prevents the sail from bellying up. When the sail is lowered, the wishbone is lowered to a horizontal position and shock cord is rigged between its arms to hold the furled sail.

Under sail she handles like a dinghy, and the lack of headsail makes for very relaxed maneuvering. The displacement hull with a board-up draft of 3 feet 4 inches, and a board-down displacement of 7 feet, is able and fast, and Hoyt has won many races in cruising-class events with the prototype. I found her very easy to sail and to maneuver, both under foresail alone when it blew over 18 knots and under full rig, and none of the conventional charter boats near us had the speed to stay with her. I understand that the addition of an engine and more cruising amenities has added enough weight to reduce the performance characteristics of the production boats (which I have not sailed), but that they still give fine cruising-boat performance.

The prototype had a center-cockpit, aft-cabin arrangement that provided plenty of room forward of the cockpit, but skimped a bit in the after cabin, which also had no head. An option is offered in the production boat of an aft-cockpit layout.

This boat has always attracted the biggest crowds at boat shows and has created tremendous interest among those who feel that there is room for something really different in cruising boats. Unfortunately many of them are bargain hunters, and the Freedom 40 is priced well up the scale for boats of comparative size.

# The Carib 41

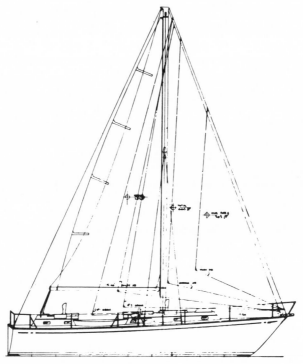

*The Carib 41.* 41' × 35' × 14' × 6'6"

While the term "breakthrough" is perhaps a bit too dramatic, the words "widely influential" and "innovative" can certainly be used to describe the impact of this Alan Gurney–designed sloop on the cruising yacht field. The enterprising New Jersey dentist, Dr. John Van Ost, who revolutionized the bareboat charter field by starting Caribbean Sailing Yachts in 1967, went through two seasons of using what stock boats there were around to fill out his fleets and then decided to get what he really wanted in a cruising boat by commissioning this design.

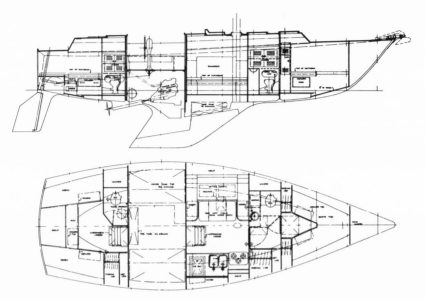

*The Carib 41.*

This desire to get the right boats for his charter fleets eventually led him beyond commissioning special designs into starting his own boat-building company, whose products are represented here by the CSY 37 (p. 111) and CSY 44 (p. 143).

The Carib 41 was the first boat to combine the elements that are now considered standard, if not obligatory, in full-cruising boats, and it was the first one to ignore completely the concept of the racer/cruiser (of which we have seen several examples) that was popular up to that time. It so happened that the introduction of the Carib 41 more or less coincided with the adoption of the IOR for ocean racing, and the two types of boats were forcibly headed on their now widely divergent paths by these simultaneous developments.

After analyzing his customers' reactions and studying the performance of boats in use, Van Ost decided he wanted a roomy, underrigged, center-cockpit boat, big enough to sleep three couples in a modicum of comfort and privacy, small enough to be handled without a crew, and able enough to make the open-water passages between islands in the Windwards and Leewards. Gurney provided a boat of 14 feet beam, carried well aft to allow for a roomy aft cabin, and a fin-keel, skeg-rudder underbody with lines that would provide adequate sailing performance and respectable speed with a forty-horsepower diesel. A special construction method of a foam-cored fiberglass sandwich provided strength, lightness, and flotation, and also helped to reduce condensation on the inside, a bugaboo in the tropics.

Innovative at the time, this method had advantages, but probably did not provide the long-lasting qualities of straight fiberglass lay-up, and it has not been used extensively after the company using it went out of business.

The rig of the Carib 41 is of very low aspect for a 41-footer, but worked well in the breezy Caribbean trade winds and was easy to handle by charterers. We took a Carib 41 for ten days from St. Vincent to Martinique and back into the Grenadines, and found her well able to stand up to trades in the high 20s with stronger gusts. The center-cockpit idea has its detractors, who feel it gets its occupants wetter going to windward, but the Carib 41, with its high freeboard and flared sheer at the bow, had no problem with this until it got rough enough to get you wet anywhere on deck.

This design lasted ten years in the CSY fleets under hard, constant use, before being retired in favor of the newer breed of CSY boats, and its influence will be felt for many more years.

# The OI 41

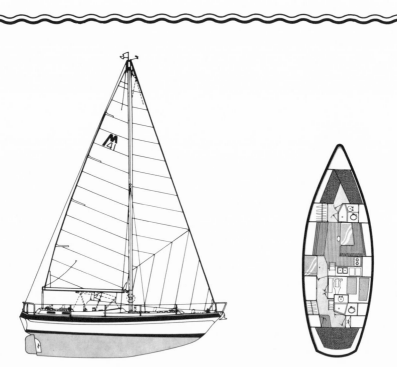

*The Morgan Out Island 41.* 41'3" × 34' × 13'10" × 4'2"

It's a good bet that more people have cruised in this design than in any other above 30 feet, as the Morgan Out Island 41 has been the most popular bareboat in Caribbean waters ever since it was introduced in 1971, and over six hundred have been built, with many, of course, also going to private owners. This was designer Charley Morgan's answer to the Carib 41 and its popularization of the center-cockpit idea for bareboating, and she was a radical departure from the current thinking when she came out, as there was no attempt made to compromise comfort with all-around sailing ability.

Living and entertaining space came first in a hull with the tremen-

140

dous beam of almost 14 feet, and the shallow, low-deadrise underbody, with a long keel, no centerboard, and 4-foot 2-inch draft, was obviously aimed at gunkholing rather than windward performance. This boat was conceived from the keel up as a cruising boat, not an adaptation of an ocean-racing mold to a cruising layout as in the OI 36, and nobody who has ever sailed one will ever claim that she is a whiz to windward. We had one for a week of Virgin Island cruising and we agreed on both counts. She is comfortable, and she manages to go to windward, but not enthusiastically. Giving her her full head at a rather wide angle to the wind, more than 50°, is the best way of eventually getting to a windward objective.

Since few charterers worry about windward performance, and every other feature fits in well with chartering requirements, the OI 41 worked out beautifully, and many different operating companies had fleets of them working. In later versions, many are still going strong in Caribbean charter fleets, and it is also one of the most frequently seen boats in every popular cruising area where private owners operate.

Some of the early models had construction problems, showing a lack of hull rigidity, but new management at Morgan upped standards and quality control, eliminating early difficulties. Privately owned OI 41s, specially adapted and outfitted, have made long transoceanic passages, and one survived a severe roll-down by a rogue wave in the North Pacific without structural damage. For passage making in favorable winds, the broad, shallow hull is a good sail-carrying platform, and the long waterline gives her a good speed potential on reaches and runs.

The early boats had no walk-through, but one was added as an option after several years, which had the effect of ruining the comfortable cockpit by raising the seat on the port side to coaming level. Standard power was specified as a 4–107, forty-horsepower diesel, but the hull can handle more power than that, and better performance is achieved with a bigger engine of fifty or more horsepower.

There is also a rig option between ketch and sloop, with better performance achieved as a single sticker, as the main is very small in the ketch rig and provides very little drive.

The big plus in this boat—and there has to be one to create such popularity—is in the really fine accommodations, with roomy forward

*The Morgan Out Island 41.*

and aft staterooms, each with head and shower, and a main saloon that can be adapted to provide as many as four bunks for those who sleep a lot of guests, but basically is a pleasantly roomy living and eating space, good for relaxing and entertaining. This feature alone has sold it to many powerboat people converting to sail, and the boat remains one of the real success stories in the cruising auxiliary field.

# The CSY 44

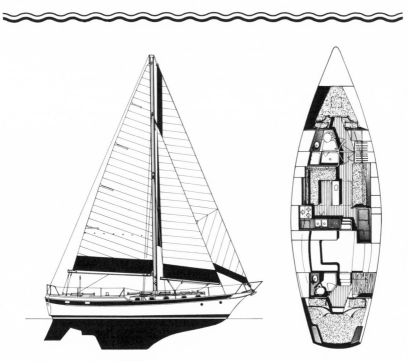

*The CSY 44.* 44' × 36'4" × 13'4" × 6'

When the Carib 41 and Pearson 390 began to reach the end of their intended use period, and the bareboat chartering business was continuing to expand, Dr. Van Ost, who had the original concept for the Carib 41, began to think about the next special boat for his burgeoning operations. After ten years of experience with charter fleets, he had developed a very full set of ideas on just what he wanted in the next boat, and he had naval architect Peter Schmitt tie them together in a formal design. His original intention was to have a stock boat manufacturer build the design for him, but this program ran into serious snags, and a sudden decision was made in October 1976 to form a company and build the boats without worrying about production problems and quality control in someone else's plant.

From that decision, with nothing in being but a design and full-production specifications, CSY was formed, a plant was found and put in commission in Tampa, a work force was hired, and the first CSY 44 hit the water in January 1977, fully found and ready to go. This I know, because we were cruising in her a few weeks later, shaking her down in Tampa Bay, and what we found was quite impressive. A later cruise in the Bay Islands of Honduras confirmed first impressions and added rough-water experience.

Van Ost and Schmitt had thought out every inch of the boat for function and practicality, still using that same concept made popular in the Carib 41, Pearson 390, OI 41, and similar boats, of a tricabin, center-cockpit arrangement without a walk-through (although this option is offered to private owners). The boat is still intended for a maximum of six people, which makes good sense, although it is at about the upper size limit of a boat that can be bareboated without crew help. Some couples might find her too big for them by themselves, although all gear is quite manageable.

Van Ost's original concept for charter boats was to keep the equipment as simple as possible, leaving off pressure water, anchor windlasses, refrigeration, and all the items that tend to go on the fritz, especially under constant use by succeeding waves of nonowners, but the competition began offering all these things, so the CSY 44 has them all too, but carefully thought out and engineered. Most of the items we have on our CSY 37 were originally developed for the 44, which preceded it by a year. The refrigeration system, once you have granted that you must run the engine for at least an hour a day, has proved very workable and does make quite a difference in "gracious living." The engine is a Perkins 4-154 diesel.

One facet Van Ost was absolutely adamant on in setting up specifications was strength of construction, and the 44 is a solidly built boat, with heavy, reliable-looking gear such as hatches, ports, locker handles, cabinets, and rigging. She too has a tremendous number of hatches and opening ports for good ventilation in the tropics.

Some charterers I have talked to have felt that the CSY 44's

*The CSY 44.*

performance is a bit sluggish, and I can understand this after my experience in comparing the performance of our CSY 37 and her custom sails against boats with the heavy, battenless chartering sails. This is a handicap on charter boats, but private owners can arrange for sails that will give livelier results. Boat Number One, which we sailed in Tampa Bay, had custom sails and gave us some good, brisk sailing, and the boat we sailed in the Bay Islands did well in a breeze and trade-wind seas even with charter sails. Private owners are also being offered a taller rig for areas with lighter winds than in chartering waters down south.

# The Morgan 45

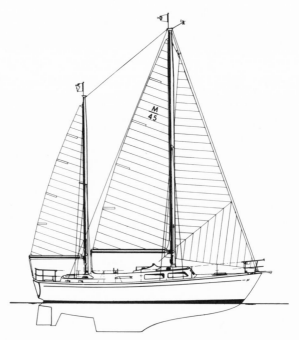

*The Morgan 45.*

This design, originally by Henry Scheel, has had a somewhat involved history. It was developed for Scheel's own company as a premium-priced, semicustom, luxury yacht, but production costs ended that venture, and Scheel sold the design to Morgan, for whom he had once worked as a house designer. By adapting it to production-line techniques, Morgan was able to cut the price almost in half, putting the boat right into a very competitive segment of the market. Then, as bareboat fleets kept expanding into bigger and bigger boats, with more elaborate equipment and more luxurious appointments, the Moorings, one of the top Virgin Islands charter companies, which had been

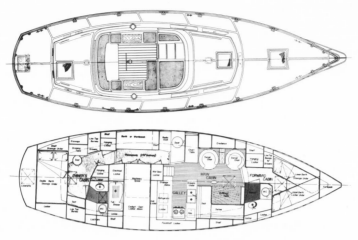

*The Morgan 45.* 45′ × 39′3″ × 13′6″ × 5′6″

getting along very well with the Morgan OI 41 and Gulfstars, decided to adapt the design to charter purposes. As altered and redesigned in layout for use by the Moorings, it became known as the Morgan 46.

The ketch version we cruised in on Florida's Biscayne Bay for a few days was the first Morgan adaptation of Scheel's original design. I thought she might be a bit big for two of us to handle, but we got along fine. On one day when it blew close to 20 knots and our course was a broad reach, we simply used jib and jigger, the major advantage of the ketch rig, and had a fine slide up Biscayne Bay from Key Largo. In air of about 14 knots on another day, we had a delightful close reach out into the Gulf Stream and back, putting her hard on the wind for a while and tacking a few times to see how she maneuvered, which was okay. In a flat calm she did about 8.5 knots under her Perkins 4-154 and the only fault I found with her under power was a certain sluggishness in response while maneuvering around slips in a crowded marina. The turning circle was rather big, and response was slow to rudder moves and throttle bursts, but added familiarity no doubt would have solved this problem.

Despite her size and the rather stately feel of having a real ship under you, her rig was not difficult to handle, especially with self-tailing winches.

*The Morgan 45.*

Living accommodations are very spacious, with an excess of head-room that makes it hard to close hatches from below. The galley is all-electric, which I'm not sure I'd want for myself since the generator must be run for cooking while away from shore power, and the boat we were on had just about every gadget known to man, even unto an ice-maker, except, for some strange reason, no power anchor windlass. I got my exercise pulling the anchor up one morning.

This model has no access directly to the deck from the after cabin, which has been changed in the adaptation by the Moorings, and an extension of the trunk cabin forward, rather than a pronounced camber in the foredeck, now takes care of headroom in the forward cabin. There is plenty of room here on an able, seaworthy hull to provide comfort in many different guises.

148

# The Cal 2-46

The "2" in the design designation is the way Jensen Marine, which builds Cal boats from Bill Lapworth designs, has of pointing out that this is a new version of a previous design of the same length. The original Cal 46, which came out in the mid-1960s, was made famous by a boat named *Fram*, which circumnavigated North America (with the help of a flatcar ride from Duluth, Minnesota, to the Pacific Northwest). The original 46 was almost purely a motor-sailer, and the redesign, which came out in 1973, puts more emphasis on sailing qualities and has a less bulky profile, improving the aesthetics.

I had the opportunity of a long weekend of cruising to Catalina, just about the only place you can cruise to from the Los Angeles area, with Lapworth and his wife Peggy, by way of introduction to this very roomy full-cruising boat. It happened that Bill had not spent much time on the boat since it had gone into production, and it was a fascinating exercise in attention to detail to see how he went over her inch by inch to see how everything was working out. I remember particularly that he happened to hit his head on a hasp for the lock on the main companionway hatch, which was hanging down from the sliding hatch. As he muttered curses and taped it up, he put a note in his memo pad to have the hasp placed on the hatch board instead of hanging down as a head knocker. Of such hundreds of minor details are good boats put together.

Despite roomy space that gave the impression of a boat 20 feet bigger, the Cal 2-46 had been planned for a party of six at most, with four a better number in two very comfortable cabins. The after cabin is practically a suite, with a big double bunk, settee, and large head, and there was an option of two single bunks instead of the double and settee. In a boat this size, with the superstructure of a motor-sailer, it makes sense to have a walk-through, as it doesn't add to the height of

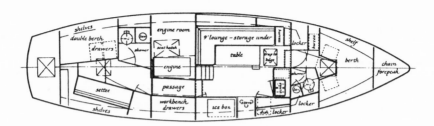

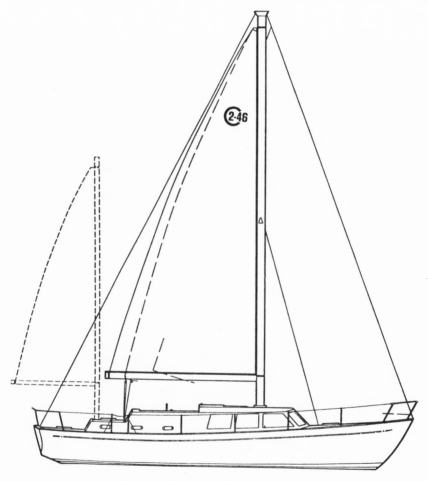

*The Cal 2-46. 45′6″ × 37′6″ × 12′6″ × 5′*

the profile or take away from what amounts to a very roomy engine compartment. Depending on how the deckhouse is laid out under the options offered, the walk-through can be a sail bin, workbench, or navigation table, or someone might want a bunk there.

The light, airy deckhouse, from which it is possible to see out while sitting down, can be arranged as an L-shaped lounge and table to port, or, in the same space, a dinette, with a navigation station forward of it. In both cases, the galley takes up the starboard side of the deckhouse with a generous amount of working space. Extra bunks can be converted from the lounge or the dinette.

The cockpit, which is intended as a fair-weather entertainment center as well as the sailing control area, is roomy and comfortable. Side decks are at a minimum for fore-and-aft access only, but the foredeck and after deck are uncluttered for sail handling and/or sunning.

As in all Lapworth boats, sailing qualities are important. The Cal 2-46 has no pretensions to racing ability, but I found that she handles on all points of sailing, tacking rather slowly due to a long keel, and fast passages have been made over long oceanic distances. The able, dry hull is easy in a heavy sea, and it moves along at over 8 knots with a Perkins 4-236 eighty-five-horsepower diesel.

# The Gulfstar Sailmaster 47

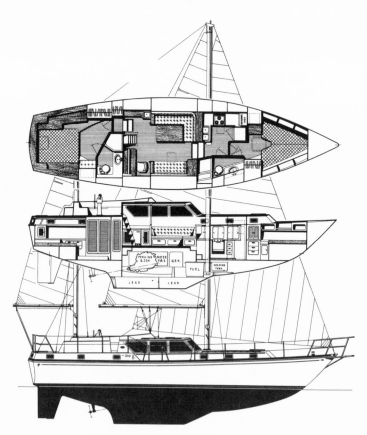

*The Gulfstar 47.* 47′ × 41′10″ × 14′2″ × 4′11″

Gulfstar's entry into the cruising auxiliary field in 1971 was with sailing motor-sailers. These established the company, and then, as the years went by, there was a trend away from this type toward straight sailing yachts. In 1977 a decision was made to return to the original concept that got the company going, and the Sailmaster 47 was introduced. It

*The Gulfstar 47.*

was based on a tested sailing hull, that of the Gulfstar 50, which had become very popular in charter operations in the Caribbean, and, slightly altered, had done respectably in ocean racing.

With a fined-down entry, slight change in the rudder, and a shortened overhang aft, the same hull was adapted to a motor-sailer layout, and the result has been that relative rarity, a motor-sailer that really sails.

153

One look at the deckhouse and raised center cockpit and there is no question that this is a boat with a great deal of room. There is powerboat-type space in the deckhouse, roomy and airy with its big windows and containing a dinette, settee, navigation station, and wet bar. This is a pleasant amenity, as pointed out, that is not included too often in auxiliaries but works wonders in keeping chaos out of the predinner happy hour. The after cabin is very large, with a big double bunk, and the head is big enough to have a separate stall shower, a nice touch for those who are tired of getting the toilet paper all wet when they take a shower in the conventional head compartment. There is also a large amount of locker space and an extra hanging locker for foul-weather gear, another amenity often lacking in boats under 50 feet.

The galley is just forward of the deckhouse saloon, with easy access, and a forward stateroom with private head, also with stall shower, completes the accommodations.

There is the other side of motor-sailer performance in the 8.5-knot cruising speed from her 6-354 Perkins diesel, which has a range of twelve hundred miles on a tankage of 195 gallons. Combined with water capacity of 300 gallons, this makes the Sailmaster self-sufficient for long periods, and a draft of 5 feet 6 inches allows her to poke into many cruising areas that are usually not available to boats of this size. Engine noise under the main saloon has been well insulated against. Access is through a big hatch.

Gulfstar has upped quality of workmanship and construction considerably since the company started, and there has been a renewed emphasis on quality first and price second. Joiner work and cabinetry is first rate, and a great deal of thought has been given to decoration. Naturally, a full range of electronic options is offered, depending on the owner's demands.

I had a good day's sail on Tampa Bay in the Gulfmaster in a fresh December norther, and she performed well on all points of sailing. A Hood Multi-Purpose Spinnaker, that company's version of the Flasher, added a great deal to her performance off the wind and right on up to a close reach. On this size boat, it is a big sail and would take some handling, but the added zip to the sailing is well worth it.

# The Olympic 47

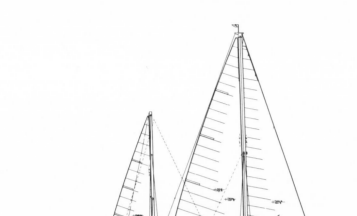

The Olympic 47.

This Ted Brewer–designed ketch was built in Greece to the best modern standards and specifications, and unfortunately has gone out of production, as she is a husky, able, and roomy boat that has proved popular with private owners, and particularly as a charter yacht in the Aegean. We had a short cruise in her out of Piraeus and found her well set up for the purpose and quite far ahead of most of the charter yachts operating in Greece in equipment, amenities, and performance. She is big enough to be comfortable for a party as large as eight, and yet is not too big to be handled by experienced sailors.

When we were aboard, she had a "shipkeeper" as crew, an ex-

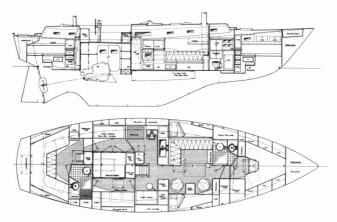

*The Olympic 47.* 47′ × 38′ × 14′3″ × 5′10″

perienced mechanic and seaman who made sure that everything was running correctly, did the routine deck and maintenance chores, and served as guide and interpreter in strange harbors. He was not the captain, however, and the charter party could make their own decisions as to destinations, sail setting and handling, and general operations. This is a good system for Greek chartering, since one of the major complaints over the years has been that the licensed "captains" of many charter yachts are merchant seamen with no experience in sail and no desire to gain any.

The Olympic 47 is well laid out for this type of operation. She has a roomy, comfortable owner's stateroom aft, with its own head, a single cabin for the professional, and lots of bunk space in the main cabin and forward stateroom. We were eight and a paid hand aboard, and there was little sense of crowding or inconvenience.

The center-cockpit layout makes for a lot of lounging room on deck, and the rig is easily handled for the most part from the cockpit. Sailing performance is fine, with good speed downwind and satisfactory windward ability, plus good speed under power with a sixty-two-horse-power Perkins diesel. She handled well in making some difficult Mediterranean-type moors, stern-to to the quay in crowded Greek harbors. Quite a few of these boats are operating in charter service in the Aegean.

# The Sou'wester 50

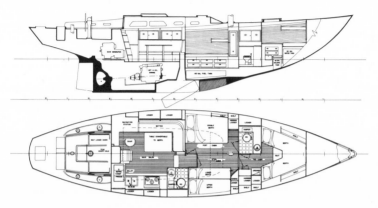

*The Hinckley 50.* 50'8" × 36'5" × 13' × 5'9"

When cost is no object and an owner wants a boat equipped with every amenity imaginable, Hinckley, as I have mentioned, usually has a boat to fit the bill. The Sou'wester 50 embodies all the extras and individual choices a demanding owner can make in a basic stock hull. There is a measure of cost saving in working from a stock hull, but from there on out, the whole approach is in a custom mode. The 50 has been offered in four different layouts, with options available on just about every piece of equipment that could be put aboard.

Layout A was a special case for one owner who wanted plenty of room for himself while discouraging guests from remaining aboard too long. It consisted of a large stateroom with a big head forward, a nonconvertible circular dinette, two pilot berths, a navigation station, and a roomy galley. Better use of a beamy 50 feet comes in the other layout options. Layout B is a tricabin affair with a big saloon taking up the after end of the cabin and containing the galley along the starboard bulkhead, a navigation station, and a convertible dinette. A passageway

*The Hinckley 50.*

leading forward has upper and lower bunks to starboard and an owner's cabin with double bunk to port. These two share a head that is just off the main saloon, and a second guest cabin with head is located forward. A variation of this layout, labeled C, substitutes a crew cabin with separate hatch to the deck forward, and layout D reverses things by putting the owner's cabin under the forward end of the cockpit, with the galley and navigation station next forward, then the main cabin containing a settee and table and upper and lower bunks, and a guest cabin ahead of that.

The model I sailed on had plan B, with an extra-large 120-horsepower Lehman-Ford diesel (80 horsepower is standard), and was completely equipped with roller-reefing gear on jib, main, and mizzen, along with electric self-tailing winches, and all halyards and sheets led to the cockpit for the greatest ease of control possible. Despite my own reservations contained in Robinson's law, all this seemed to work quite well, and certainly made for ease and efficiency in handling a boat of this size. There was a bit of a problem with unrolling the main until all the lines were unkinked and led free, and straightness of the mast is a key element in the success of this system from Hood Yacht Systems. If the mast is out of true, the sail can bunch up and jam in the slot going in or out.

These were roller-reefing sails, which means that they can be used with any area exposed that seems right, as opposed to roller furling, in which the sail must be used at full size or not at all.

Despite the profusion of gear, the deck and cockpit layout was clean and uncluttered, and I have never been on a 50-footer that was easier to handle. Contrary to the usual limitations, a reasonably agile couple could handle this rig quite well (as long as all the gadgets are in working order).

There was the usual full complement of electronic gear found on most Hinckleys; the cabin decor was light and airy, with the traditional teak and holly cabin sole as part of it; tankage of 300 gallons for fuel and 280 for water meant a good cruising range; and an extra touch of thoughtfulness was a mast height of 62 feet for Intracoastal Waterway bridge clearance. A Luke automatic feathering propeller seemed to give good control, and "weathervanes" to cut down drag when under sail.

# The Gallant 53

Like the smaller Excalibur 36 of a few years before, this ketch was also designed by the Dutch naval architect Van de Stadt (see also the Oceans 71, p. 165), and we had a cruise in her in 1968 from Martinique to Grenada, with a professional captain and deckhand. This was a time when it was the thing to do to adapt fast ocean racers to the charter service, and this boat was the latest thing in a modern ocean racer at the time. She had made a fast passage across from Europe to join the Caribbean charter fleet, and a sloop-rigged sister ship was the first stock boat in the 1968 single-handed Transatlantic Race.

An ocean racer then could still have private, paneled cabins and many electronic amenities, and she was actually equipped with air conditioning. This sounded good for nights spent in a slip, when the breeze might not come through the cabin at the proper angle as when riding at anchor. It turned out, however, that air conditioning put too much of a load on the vessel's circuits, and it never seemed to get turned on, which was all right with us.

She was comfortable for four in our charter party and a crew of two—although the Bequia-born deckhand much preferred to sleep on deck no matter how much room there was below—but there was a sense of overcrowding or lack of space below since, in the British fashion, everything was cut up into rather small compartments.

There was a real dividend in her sailing ability, though. This was before the days of permanently rigged Bimini tops, which now seem like an absolute must for me for tropical cruising, but she was such a lively, able sailer that we could do without the mizzen very easily, leaving an awning rigged over its boom, and still have some exhilarating sailing reaching across the trades on interisland passages. In previous Caribbean crewed charters we had been on a 1903 schooner and a converted North Sea trawler, and the contrast between their stately

*The Gallant 53.* 53'2" × 38'8" × 13'1" × 7'4"

progress and the exciting sailing in the Gallant 53 was startling.

This trend to good sailing quality in crewed charter boats, which was just beginning at the time of this cruise, superseding the North Sea conversions, Brixham trawlers, and ancient luxury schooners, continued through the 1970s, and an inspection trip I made to the St. Thomas charter boat fleet in the winter of 1978–9 revealed, in a fleet of over a hundred boats, almost total conversion to modern, well-designed boats with real sailing ability, not ocean racers anymore, but cruising boats with a good turn of speed.

# The Herreshoff 58

Amid all the modern fiberglass vessels and stock boats that have been discussed here, the 58-foot L. Francis Herreshoff ketch *Circe* is a throwback to ancient times. Really a custom boat, and a design dating back to the 1930s, she is mainly of historical interest, but I include her here as an example of a fast-disappearing breed, a lovely, traditional, wooden yacht with fine sailing ability, a joy to look at and to be aboard for a number of reasons.

We had two experiences with *Circe*. She was the means of our first cruise in the Virgin Islands back in 1964, before there were any bareboats and when the professionally crewed yachts could be counted on your fingers and toes (plus maybe a few more) and were a mixed bag of relics going back into the nineteenth century. Then, in 1970, when she had left chartering and gone to a private owner, I was invited to be her skipper in her owner's absence in the 'Round Grenada Race.

Her design came from Herreshoff's original *Tioga* for the Noyes family of Marblehead, Massachusetts, and presaged his design for the same family's next *Tioga*, a 72-foot ketch that became famous as *Ticonderoga* under later owners. Both designs came from the 1930s, and there is a distinct kinship in looks between them, with a lovely sheer, clipper bow and graceful counter stern and overhang aft. This long, slender hull went right back to the clipper ship era in its traditions, and I don't know of any handsomer sailing yachts. *Circe* and *Ticonderoga* are both going strong into the 1980s, and it's good to have them around as reminders, and as wonderful boats to sail in when the chance comes.

*Circe* was almost new when we cruised in her in the Virgins, as she had been custom built in the Balearic Islands in Spain expressly for Caribbean chartering, and great tender loving care had gone into her construction. Her joinerwork showed fine, old-world craftsmanship and

*The Herreshoff 58 Circe. 58' × 49'6" × 13'1" × 6'6"*

her interior woods had been carefully chosen and matched for a very pleasing, light, and attractive below-decks feeling. Just one miscalculation had been made. In a rather common mistake in adapting a boat for charter service, her guest bunks, consisting of uppers and lowers, had too little space between them, and sleeping was a bit difficult and claustrophobic, with poor ventilation.

This was a small price to pay for the glorious sails we had in her as she put her rail down and responded to the fresh trades. This was a ship under you, a long-keeled, steady, powerful hull that fit the water beautifully and transmitted a real sense of power as she surged along. Would that there were more like her.

164

# The Oceans 71

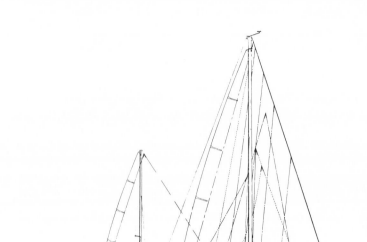

*The Ocean 71.*

This maxi ocean racer is a fiberglass version of the famous Van de Stadt–designed ketch *Stormvogel*, one of the most widely raced and cruised yachts in the history of the sport. *Stormvogel*, a lean, slender, canoe-shaped speedster, was built of molded plywood since her owner was in the plywood business, and the design was adapted for fiberglass construction and produced as a stock boat in England by the same company that built the Gallant 53. We had a charter cruise in one in the Grenadines in 1972, reveling in the luxury of service by a crew of four and in exciting big-boat performance.

This was made particularly graphic for us in sailing by Kick 'em Jenny, the notorious rock off Grenada where we had taken a real

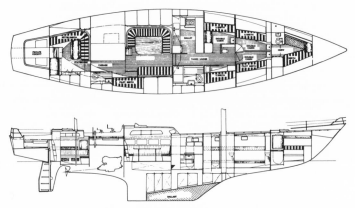

*The Ocean 71.* 71' × 56' × 17'4" × 8'

dusting in smaller boats like the Excalibur 36 and Hughes 38. The trade wind was just as boisterous on the January day we sailed by it in the Oceans 71, and the big blue rollers were sweeping in just as majestically from the open Atlantic to the Caribbean, but we rode serenely dry in the cockpit while a bit of spray dashing across the hull near the mast was the only reminder of where we were.

Naturally, there was plenty of room aboard for our party of four, with some to spare, and the deck and cockpit were also roomy and comfortable, with plenty of space for lounging, sunning, and moving around. For a boat of this size the rig was not too hard to handle as it was split well between the main and mizzen, but it was good to have a crew to do the major part of the work. She could handle up to 30 knots without shortening down the main or mizzen, carrying a good-size jib, with a real feeling of stability and power.

There was just one drawback. When her owners decided to put her into charter service, they converted her layout to include two double cabins, one on each side of a passageway, aft of the roomy main saloon. The bunks consisted of an upper and a slightly wider lower, but the space between them was so small that it was impossible to turn over while lying in the bottom bunk, a much more confined space than in *Circe.* This also meant that there was very little air, a severe problem in the tropics. I spent about ten claustrophobic minutes in the lower the first night aboard and then quickly came out for air. Somehow Jane and I both managed to sleep in the upper from then on, a bit crowded, but better than the coffin-like feeling in the lower. This, I'm sure, was corrected fairly soon, and I believe was a feature of that individual boat, not a characteristic of all Oceans 71s, which can be finished off with any custom layout an owner desires.

# The Rhodes 72 Ketch

*The Rhodes 72-foot ketch* Barlovento.

Up in this range there aren't exactly stock boats anymore (although the Alden 75 [p. 171] is a stock hull). *Barlovento,* P. S. duPont's Rhodes-designed ketch, is a custom steel boat built at Abeking & Rasmussen in Germany, but she is very representative of a type that Phil Rhodes turned out in varying sizes that achieved wide recognition as luxurious maxi yachts. On very much the same lines, there was a class of Rhodes 77 ketches that combined real luxury with fine sailing ability, and quite a few were built.

*Barlovento,* built in 1959, and still going strong and in top-notch condition, is very similar to the 77s in concept, but was scaled down

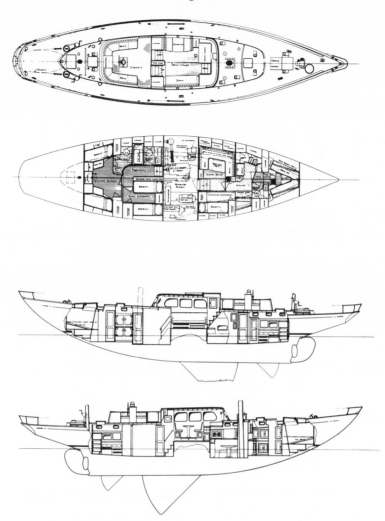

*The Rhodes 72-foot ketch* Barlovento. 71'8″ × 50' × 18' × 5'6″

to the 72-foot range to qualify for the Bermuda Race, which she has entered many times. I was in her crew in 1960 when she charged through the worst storm ever to hit the race, carrying a full main and staysail through the wild night before the finish, to take fourth prize in Class A.

Although she has raced a great deal and has won her share of prizes when it blows hard (she is a heavy boat that needs a breeze to get her moving), she is basically a comfortable cruising boat, used extensively by her owner and family in New England, the Chesapeake, and southern waters. As a centerboarder, she has a board-up draft of just 5 feet 6 inches, which opens up many areas of the Bahamas normally denied to boats of this size. In addition to her main centerboard, she has a trimming board just forward of the rudder which adds greatly to her steering stability and makes her easy to control in the roughest going. When she settles into a groove on a breezy reach or run, she is like a locomotive on a track. Her broad hull is extremely powerful under the right conditions, but her long, graceful overhangs give her a waterline of 50 feet, quite short for a 72-footer, cutting down on her maximum hull-speed potential compared to other "maxis."

Although her appointments are luxurious, *Barlovento* is not designed to carry a crowd for cruising. There are crew bunks for three in the forward compartment, but the owner's quarters only has two staterooms, each with a head, and there is one bathtub that can be entered from either head (it makes a great place for stowing foul-weather gear in rough going). Guest capacity can be expanded by using the sofa and dinette in the large, airy deckhouse, which is fine for entertaining. The dining area, down a steep ladder forward of the deckhouse, is not very spacious and a bit dark, but handy to the galley, which is adjacent to the crew's quarters. A large engine room under the deckhouse runs the full width of the vessel, where the GM 4-71 main engine, generator, and other auxiliary equipment are located.

*Barlovento* remains one of the best examples still in commission of a classic Rhodes concept.

# The Alden 75

*The Alden/Palmer Johnson 75 ketch* MaMu V.

This is a stock boat? Well, in a manner of speaking it is, since the hull is stock and standard, but from there on up an owner who can afford this type of yacht can also expect to have the accommodations customized to his own requirements. She recalls the Rhodes 77s of the 1940s in this treatment, and in her general category of an auxiliary with the maximum in comfortable accommodations and equipment for long-range cruising combined with real sailing ability in a vessel that looks like a sailboat.

I had a day and a night out of Chicago aboard *MaMu V* to get an idea of how all this fits together. The boat had been beautifully built

*The Alden/Palmer Johnson 75 ketch* MaMu V. 75' × 57' × 18' × 6'6"

in aluminum by the Palmer Johnson Yard in Sturgeon Bay, Wisconsin, and was still more or less on shakedown when we headed out on a mirror-calm Lake Michigan in hopes of getting an idea of her sailing ability. Actually, seeing her perform in light zephyrs was perhaps more revealing than a whole-sail breeze, as she ghosted along remarkably well for a boat with such a full complement of amenities.

She answered her helm well and went through tacks and jibes without coaxing, and as she got moving she built her own apparent wind and carried a good momentum. Also, the tall rig of a 75-footer helps to pick up air above the surface that might not be detectable right at water level. Later on, she entered the Chicago-Mackinac Race and charged along impressively at the head of the fleet as long as the good breeze that boosted her away from the start lasted.

Needless to say, her accommodations are as luxurious as anyone would want, with a large owner's stateroom aft and two absolutely identical guest cabins forward of it in the passageway to the deckhouse —no protocol problems here about which guest got the better cabin. The 13- by 13-foot deckhouse is finished in varnished teak, with plenty of lounging space, a handsome desk, and a wet bar. In general, vinyls and Formicas are used on bulkheads and in service areas for ease of maintenance. The galley and dining area are down and forward of the deckhouse, with a crew's quarters ahead of them. The galley is big enough for ease of operation in port but compact enough for security at sea, and cooking is by electricity.

This, along with all the other electronics that might be expected, means that a big engine room is needed for the Volvo TAMD 70C 270-horsepower diesel and Onan fifteen-kilowatt, 110/220-volt a.c.

*The Alden/Palmer Johnson 75 ketch* MaMu V.

generator, and a Maxim HJ-3 water maker. Tankage is for 1800 gallons of fuel and 990 of water.

She is a centerboarder, and a draft of 6 feet 6 inches with board up opens a wide horizon of shallow-water cruising areas normally denied a maxi like this. The board is hydraulically operated.

With all this equipment and living space, she is still big enough to be nicely proportioned, with long graceful overhangs, a pleasing sheer line, and a cabin trunk and pilot house that do not bulk too large. The rig is a real sailing one, not a motor-sailer makeshift, and all in all she represents about the finest in sailing yachts now available.

# *Schooner* America *Replica*

THE SCHOONER YACHT, AMERICA, 170 TONS

BUILT BY Mᴿ STEERS TO J. C. STEVENS ESQᴿᴱ COMMODORE OF THE NEW YORK YACHT CLUB

This isn't exactly your run-of-the-mill, everyday cruising yacht. In fact she is a unique, one-off recreation of the most historic yacht in America, if not the world. She was built in 1967 from Sparkman & Stephens adaptations of the lines of the original *America* to be the star of a TV documentary about *America* and the cup she brought home from England in 1851. With her name on it, the New York Yacht Club has held the cup ever since, the longest winning streak in sports history in the oldest international event in sports.

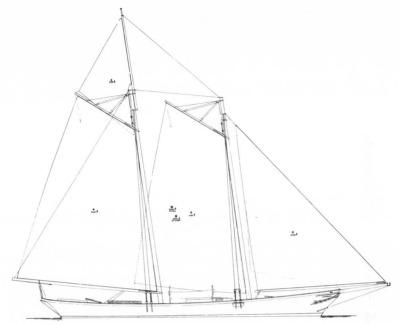

*The 103-foot replica of the schooner* America. 103′ × 90′3″ × 22′ × 11′

I was lucky enough to sail in the replica in Op Sail '74 in the Baltic, when she was owned as a private yacht by Pres Blake of Springfield, Massachusetts. He had cruised her over there, and later brought her back via Africa. It was one of the thrills of a sailing lifetime to charge across a gray, rainy Baltic at about 14 knots on a broad reach in this 103-foot schooner. Her wake was so smooth, and she slipped through the water with so little fuss, that you had to look directly down into the water to get an idea of how fast she was going.

Blake sold her two years later, and she has since gone through several changes of ownership. One owner tried to put her in the charter business, but the basic problem is that she is a highly impractical, romantic dream. It takes a crew of a dozen or so to operate her, even with electric winches for her halyards and other modern conveniences, and her accommodations are extremely limited. On deck she is a faithful replica of an 1851 schooner, but below she is a comfortable modern yacht with just two staterooms in the owner's quarters and a large saloon that is fine for entertaining. A couple of bunks can be made

*The 103-foot replica of the schooner* America.

up here, but she is not set up to sleep a big crowd of guests, and the only way she can be operated is by someone who can afford to keep her going as a private yacht.

To see her is to get a real feeling of a long-departed era, and to sail in her is a never-to-be-forgotten experience. She is a long way up the scale from the 18-foot catboat that started this section, but both are reminders of a wonderful sailing tradition.

# Part III

Where to Cruise

Where can the boats be used?

On the following pages, there is a rundown and capsule of the cruising areas I know personally, with one or two reports based on the experiences of others. Somehow I have missed the Gulf of California and the Bras d'Or Lakes in my travels, but the others I do know. As I have pointed out, these are not the detailed instructions of a cruising guide which you hold in your lap while entering a harbor. Such instructions change yearly, and the annually issued cruising guides referred to on each area should be used when actually operating there.

Here, my intent is to give you a general idea of what each area is like, when to go there, what kind of cruising to expect, with some comments on unusual features, favorite ports, and other pertinent information that does not change too rapidly. I am frequently asked which area is my favorite, and an honest answer would probably be the place where I have most recently completed a cruise. There are so many good ones, and we have had delightful experiences in all of them. I have often said that, on being told that I had but one more cruise to make, it would be a tough choice between the Exumas and the Grenadines, as both of them have provided ideal cruising many times, but a pause to think after making a statement like that brings the realization that this is not being fair to many other areas. Let's just say that I have not included any bad ones in the following pages. We have had a great time in just about every one of them.

I have gone into specific detail on areas of the continental United States and have also included the Bahamas and Caribbean in these summaries because so many American yachtsmen go there. There is also a general rundown of foreign areas with which I am personally familiar.

Where cruising guides to these areas have been published, they are listed. (Full bibliographic information on each book can be found in the Bibliography, at the back of this book.) Note that some of these books are out-of-print, and thus can be found only in libraries or through dealers in out-of-print books.

# The Maine Coast

| | |
|---|---|
| AREA: | 45° to 46°N    68° to 70°W |
| | 200 miles, southwest-northeast |
| SEASON: | June through September |
| PREVAILING BREEZE: | Southwest |
| CLIMATE: | Cool and bracing |
| DRAFT LIMITS: | Not a factor |
| TIDAL RANGE: | 10–15 feet |
| NUMBER OF ANCHORAGES: | Inexhaustable |
| DRAWBACKS: | High percentage of fog, cold water, short season, limited facilities |
| PLUS FACTORS: | Unlimited anchorages, uncrowded, magnificent scenery, fishing |
| BOOKS: | *Waterway Guide* (annual, Northeast edition); *Cruising Guide to the New England Coast; Ranging the Maine Coast* |

There are many sailors who don't care where they cruise so long as it's Maine. The Maine Coast has an incredible number of bays, coves, rivers, inlets, cuts, thoroughfares, and passages that make it a cruising ground of infinite opportunity, and it has fostered some of the most fanatical loyalty of any cruising area anywhere. These "Maineiacs" all have a deep-down feeling that Maine is really just for them and that everyone else is an intruder. They practically froth at the mouth when they see another sail on even the distant horizon, and they act like someone whose daughter has been raped if they come into a favorite "secret" cove and find another boat at anchor.

Until not too long ago this state of mind was not an unreasonable one, as there is so much to the Maine Coast that a great many boats

179

*Somes Sound, Mt. Desert Island, Maine.*

can be spread rather thinly all along it and not impinge on each other's privacy. With the growth in cruising participation in all waters in recent years, Maine too has become more populated, but this is only in a comparative sense—comparative, that is, to the almost complete isolation and privacy that was enjoyed a generation ago. In another comparative sense, placing it against the waters to the south of Cape Cod, or farther away in places like the Virgins and Chesapeake, it is still very uncrowded. I have spent entire days cruising in the Mount Desert–Blue Hill area and seen perhaps half a dozen other boats on a day of good sailing conditions, and the only harbors that become crowded are in the busier centers like Boothbay, Camden, and Northeast. You may find other boats in the secluded anchorages, but you won't be fighting for mooring room from 1500 on. There is plenty of room for all who want to cruise in Maine, and no one person could possibly spend a night in all the anchorages there are in a lifetime of cruising seasons, although some dedicated fanatics have come fairly close.

There is a catch to that phrase "a lifetime of cruising seasons"; in other words, the Maine season is fairly short, which is one of the drawbacks. Mid-June to mid-September is about the extent of it for reasonable expectations of good conditions, although there are those who push it a bit at both ends. And in any season there are quite a few days that are lost to fog. Fog is an ever-present fact of life along the Maine Coast, which is a natural fog factory. The ingredients that produce this situation are icily cold water—in the low fifties at best even in mid-summer—combined with warm air coming off the great land mass of North America. When these elements clash, with the right amount of moisture in the air, the result is instant fog, and anyone who cruises here has to be prepared for it at all times. Depending on where you are and how much you enjoy testing your navigational skills by poking your way through it, fog may or may not hamper operations. Very often, nearby there will be some waterway heading inland that connects with the next bay or river via a cut behind an island, or a maze of channels threading through the forests, and a change of scenery can at least be effected even though offshore conditions are not conducive.

Also the fog line is often just along the outer coast, in the nearby islands and at the tips of points and peninsulas.

Because of fog, and other natural features, the cruising sailor is pretty much on his own in Maine. Tidal ranges are high all along the coast, since the Gulf of Maine, with the Bay of Fundy at its northeastern end, is a large embayment that creates bigger and bigger ranges as the tides from the open sea are forced into narrowing waters. The state of the tide must be checked at all times, both while underway and at anchor. As a result of a piloting error I have been known to sail across an area that was colored green on the chart, fortunately at high tide with 10 feet of water under me, but it is an embarrassing situation to have anchored snugly at high tide only to find no water left beneath the boat when the tide goes out. (I'm not guilty of this one, but I've seen it happen.) The natural companion of big tidal ranges is strong tidal currents, and there are many places where these must be carefully considered. In some places, such as a spot called Hell Gate on the Sasanoa River, which connects the Kennebec and the Sheepscot, the current can be strong enough to prevent passage by a low-powered auxiliary.

Because of the tide range and the relative lack of population, there are very few conventional marinas in Maine, and the ones there must have floating piers. Anchoring out is standard in most places, with the tidal range and current flow always a consideration; supplies are not as readily available as in some areas, so self-sufficiency is the word. Dinghy operation must be carried on carefully. You can leave a dink on the beach at low tide and find it gone when you come back, or in the reverse situation, it might be several hundred feet from the water if it was left at the high-tide line.

These cautions might sound like a negative report on Maine cruising, but the true Maine-iac considers them as normal situations, all part of the stimulating challenge that cruising in Maine can be. It is not a dangerous area for anyone using the right amount of prudent seamanship, and the rewards can be great. There is an atmosphere that is unique in the cruising world, a heady combination of salt sea and north woods, with magnificent scenery as a backdrop. Pine-covered

*Southwest Harbor and Somes Sound, Maine.*

promontories with a rocky shoreline, offshore islands indented with secluded harbors, villages that still validly qualify for the adjective "quaint," and real mountains in the blue distance inland are all part of the picture. Maine is the only place on the eastern coast of the United States where mountains are close to the sea. Cadillac Mountain on Mount Desert Island, at 1532 feet, is the highest place on the Atlantic Coast between Labrador and Mexico. South of it, there is nothing taller than a sand dune or a high-rise hotel in Atlantic City or Miami, except for a 276-foot-high hill in the Highlands of the Navesink at the southern end of New York Harbor's Lower Bay.

In outlining sample itineraries for a Maine Coast cruise, a suggested one from the Portland area to Mount Desert could have ten variations, each giving a good harbor for the night, without duplication. One general piece of advice that Maine experts practice themselves is "Whenever you come out of a Maine harbor, turn to port." In other words, head eastward for progressively better cruising conditions. In one week it is possible to cover the eighty-five miles of crow-flight distance between Portland and Mount Desert with a great choice of stops each night, but two or three weeks could just as profitably be spent in the same area. East of Mount Desert the coast has fewer harbors and is more open and rugged, but many devoted Maine cruising people now feel that this is the only place to find peace and solitude. Beyond Schoodic Head, the next major promontory east of Mount Desert, there are longer stretches of coast without a good anchorage, and any that do exist are likely to be less well populated than those to the west.

Every Maine cruising addict of the type who comes back season after season has his own special private hideaways whose existence he guards with jealousy and secrecy, and if I had some myself I probably would not put them in print. There are, though, a number of harbors that any cruising visitor should see if possible. The busy ones I have mentioned like Boothbay, Camden, and Northeast Harbor are all busy because they are attractive and also have good facilities, and they merit a stop if only for the availability of supplies and shoreside amenities in the form of restaurants and shops. Somes Sound, which cuts deeply into

Mount Desert Island (classified as the only fjord on the east coast of the United States), is a scenic highlight and also has several excellent anchorages, such as Valley Cove. Mount Desert has many pleasant harbors around its perimeter in addition to Somes Sound and Northeast. Southwest is a bustling yachting, fishing, and commercial port; Bar Harbor is the biggest settlement; and Pretty Marsh is aptly named. Just offshore, Burnt Coat Harbor on Swans Island is one of the best in Maine.

Among the other harbors I have enjoyed are Christmas Cove, Friendship, Damariscotta, South Bristol, South Freeport, and Carver's Harbor on Vinalhaven—and that's only scratching the surface of what Maine has to offer. Come fog or high tide, it is one of the prime cruising grounds in North America.

*Nantucket Harbor.*

# Southern New England

| | |
|---|---|
| AREA: | 41° 10′ to 41° 45′ N    70° to 71° 40′ W |
| | 70 by 35 miles |
| SEASON: | Late May to mid-October |
| PREVAILING BREEZE: | Southwest |
| CLIMATE: | Pleasantly warm |
| DRAFT LIMITS: | Unlimited for 6 feet; above that, major harbors only |
| TIDAL RANGE: | 2–4 feet |
| NUMBER OF ANCHORAGES: | Over two dozen |
| DRAWBACKS: | Fog, crowding of facilities and anchorages in season, shoals and strong tides |
| PLUS FACTORS: | Reliable breezes, attractive scenery and towns, good harbors, good swimming, fishing |
| BOOKS: | *Waterway Guide* (annual, Northeast edition); *Cruising Guide to the New England Coast; Cape Cod: Where to Go* |

The other great cruising area in New England besides the Maine Coast lies south of Cape Cod and takes in the offshore islands of Nantucket, Martha's Vineyard, the Elizabeth Islands, and Block Island, as well as the many cruising stops in Narragansett Bay, in Buzzards Bay, and on the south shore of Cape Cod. Between Maine and the cape, Massachusetts Bay and Cape Cod Bay have many harbors, but most of these are highly civilized and developed, and Boston's urban sprawl dominates the center of the area. Because of this, cruising opportunities there are limited, although thousands of boats base in the waters between Maine and the cape. They race and weekend out of home ports, but they head down east to Maine or through the Cape Cod Canal to the islands when they set off on a serious cruise.

*The Nantucket Harbor.*

Physically, the area south of the cape is very different from Maine in atmosphere and in the lay of the land. Gone are the rocky shores covered with pines, and there are no mountains within view from anywhere along this coast. The shores are low and covered with scrub pines and bayberry for the most part, and the highest land is in the sandy bluffs that rise above the beaches and galloping dunes. It is just as well that there are few rocks in the area because the waters are much shallower than along the Maine Coast, and it is not hard to run aground on the many sandbars and shoals that are scattered through the whole complex of sounds, bays, and harbors. Tidal currents are still strong and very much to be reckoned with, especially in the cuts between the Elizabeth Islands and in and out of the major bodies of water.

The season is a bit longer here, with late May to early October offering a good chance for pleasant cruising, although fog is very much a factor, especially in spring when the water is still cold. It can sweep in from offshore waters at any time during the summer, however, often

188

*The Nantucket Boat Basin.*

with very little warning, and a careful navigational check should be maintained at all times. The prevailing summer breeze is southwest, building to a husky 16–18 knots on most fair afternoons, and it is often smoky, limiting visibility to a couple of miles. All this is a matter of percentages. A lucky visitor might have a whole week of fresh, warm sou'westers, or perhaps a rare, gorgeous three-day nor'easter, and the following week may bring steady fog and drizzle.

There is a wide choice of harbors, and many of the towns are steeped in atmosphere, with Nantucket, Edgartown, Menemsha, Cuttyhunk, and Marion among the most picturesque. As cruising has grown in popularity, these towns have also become more and more crowded, with great pressure on facilities for visitors at the height of the season in July and August. An owner who knows his schedule well ahead of time would be advised to make advance reservations at marinas in these and other harbors, working from one of the annual cruising guides that give specific information, phone numbers, and mailing addresses. For the skipper who likes to proceed as the spirit moves,

*A quiet harbor on the south shore of Cape Cod.*

deciding each day what the next stop will be depending on wind, weather, and the mood of the crew, taking pot luck in these popular harbors usually means anchoring out, often at a good distance from shore, and sometimes even this is hard to do properly if you arrive after the middle of the afternoon.

Most of these harbors now have public launch service for a fee, as well as some form of garbage service. Nantucket and Edgartown, for example, have garbage boats that will remove your trash for a fee, while Marion has a raft in the middle of the harbor loaded with cans where all visitors are supposed to deposit their garbage.

As far as I know, there are no hideaways left in this area. Solitude at anchor is a thing of the past, unless you have a shallow enough draft and a good enough piloting eye to poke into Chappaquiddick Pond on the Vineyard, or up Wauwinet Harbor to the eastward of Nantucket's main harbor. In my early cruising days Cuttyhunk, at the outer end of the Elizabeth Islands, was almost a secret harbor, known as a quiet retreat to the merest few experienced cruising people. Now, if you're

*Wianno, Cape Cod.*

not in there by midafternoon at the latest, there is no more room to swing at anchor.

These may seem like negative recommendations, yet the basic charm is still there, the atmosphere is very conducive to relaxing afloat, there is just the right amount of challenge in the tides, shoals, and fresh breezes, and it is still a top favorite cruising area with a great many people, including me.

The harbors I have mentioned are the obvious highlights, but there is a wide enough choice to keep you coming back for many a season without duplication and repetition. For boats basing on the mainland near here, one week is enough time for a rewarding cruise, although two would be better. Coming from further away, from New York or Boston, it would be wise to spend a long weekend getting near the area in preparation for a full-time cruise of a week or two. A growing practice is to charter a boat based in the area. There is no organized fleet chartering as in southern waters (the season is too short to support such an operation), but many owners make their boats available for individual charters through local brokers.

Coming from the west, Block Island is an obvious first stop after leaving Long Island Sound, and its Great Salt Pond is big enough to absorb a tremendous number of anchored boats, although the marinas here tend to be overwhelmed at busy times. Block is an interesting outpost of rugged individuality among its few hundred permanent residents, and there is a real feeling of being off at sea on its barren moors. A local phenomenon that often keeps timid sailors in harbor here unnecessarily is the fact that the breeze, especially the prevailing sou'wester, always seems to be blowing harder inside the harbor than it actually is outside (this is probably a thermal effect off the hills surrounding the harbor, particularly on warm days). Block Island is also a famous fog factory, especially early in the season, but no cruising yachtsman should miss it.

Along the Rhode Island mainland, it is a straight stretch of seventeen miles from the eastern end of Long Island Sound to Point Judith at the western entrance to Narragansett Bay, a good route for those who worry about being weathered in at Block. Narragansett Bay itself is a pleasant cruising ground, although its shores are now heavily populated and almost fully developed. There are many harbors, with Newport the number one attraction. It has fine facilities, good protection, many good restaurants, and all sorts of sightseeing opportunities in the mammoth "cottages" of its plush society era and the restored colonial houses near the waterfront. It is especially exciting in an America's Cup year or when such major events as the Bermuda Race or New York Yacht Club Cruise are taking place.

Bristol, Warren, East Greenwich, Jamestown, and Sakonnet are some of the good Narragansett harbors, and there are odd coves here and there where a measure of privacy can still be found if you are lucky.

Buzzards Bay is famous for some of the most consistent sailing breezes on the Atlantic Coast, since the mainland behind it seems to bring a good southwest thermal in every afternoon in normal summer weather. The breeze here probably has 5 or more knots of extra heft over the velocities in nearby bodies of water on an average summer day. When it is blowing against an ebb tide, the chop can be short and steep, but few areas provide steadier, more satisfying sailing than this

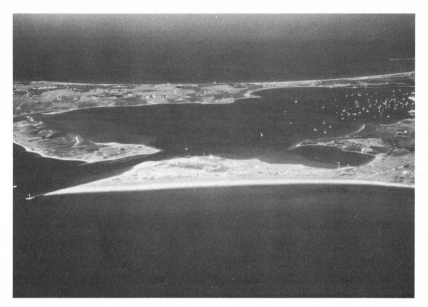

*Great Salt Pond, Block Island.*

funnel-shaped bay between Cape Cod and the mainland. Quisset, South Dartmouth, Mattapoisett, and Marion are the best harbors.

In the Elizabeth Islands that separate Buzzards Bay from Vineyard Sound, Cuttyhunk, if you can get in, is a colorful spot, and Hadley Harbor on Naushon is lovely, unspoiled on shore and well protected. The island is privately owned and landing is only allowed in specified picnic areas. The cuts or "holes" that run between Buzzards Bay and Vineyard Sound, separating the Elizabeths, are notorious for heavy tidal currents, especially Woods Hole.

Tarpaulin Cove on the Vineyard Sound side of Naushon is a fine day anchorage and all right for the night in settled weather, but beware a nor'easter here. Menemsha and Lake Tashmoo on the Vineyard are colorful and attractive, and Vineyard Haven manages to take care of a great many boats in hospitable fashion, more pleasantly than Edgartown where the visitor is exploited by the local yards and pretty much left to fend for himself. The south shore of the cape has a string of good harbors, varying in draft requirements, in Falmouth, the Centerville

*Woods Hole, Massachusetts.*

area, Hyannis, Harwichport, and Stage Harbor. All are well worth a visit.

Nantucket is the top attraction of the whole area, a beautiful old town that is an architectural rarity with over four hundred houses from the mid-nineteenth century or earlier, all sorts of restaurants, whaling museums, art galleries and shops, and miles and miles of ocean beaches beyond its windswept moors. The marina here is a big, attractive, beautifully run one, so popular that reservations for slips must be made well in advance during the two busy summer months. A word of caution on Nantucket: Its harbor is normally well protected except in a nor'easter, when it is wide open to a six-mile sweep down Wauwinet Harbor. Despite this warning, it is not to be missed, the true highlight of a marvelous cruising area.

194

# Long Island Sound

| | |
|---|---|
| AREA: | 41°N    71° 50' to 73° 50'W |
| | 100 miles, east-west |
| SEASON: | May to mid-October |
| PREVAILING BREEZE: | Variable |
| CLIMATE: | Warm |
| DRAFT LIMITS: | Not a factor in most harbors |
| TIDAL RANGE: | 5–7 feet |
| NUMBER OF ANCHORAGES: | Dozens |
| DRAWBACKS: | Lack of wind, crowding, powerboat wakes, poor water quality |
| PLUS FACTORS: | Multiple choice of anchorages, good facilities, high standard of boats and activities, fair fishing |
| BOOKS: | *Waterway Guide* (annual, Northeast edition); *Cruising Guide to the New England Coast; Where to Go . . . on Long Island Sound* |

In number of boats based there, Long Island Sound is the yachting capital of the Atlantic Coast, if not the whole country. In its hundred-mile length, it is jam-packed with good harbors, and they are all jam-packed with boats. The only barren stretch of shore is from Port Jefferson eastward along the north shore of Long Island to Orient Point. There is only one small harbor here, Mattituck Inlet, but everywhere else on the sound there is a profusion of harbors, coves, and bays.

Looking at a chart, this would seem like ideal cruising country, and in some ways it can be, but there are practical considerations that detract from this theory. For one thing, most harbors are so full of locally based boats that it is hard for visitors to find mooring, berthing, or even anchoring space. There is very little sense of escape in poking one's bow into the average Long Island harbor. The other problem is the weather, or at least the wind conditions. Even its most devoted adherents have to admit that the sound justly deserves its nickname of "The Dead Sea," at least in the summer months when everyone wants to be afloat. There is a notorious lack of wind on the average summer day, as the land mass of Long Island separates the sound from the Atlantic Ocean where sea breezes are generated as afternoon thermals, sucked into the void left by hot air rising over the land.

While the afternoon breeze comes in off the Atlantic at about noon on Great South Bay on the south side of Long Island or along the New Jersey shore, it takes longer to fight its way across the island to the sound. Oldtimers will tell you that before World War II it was the usual thing for the breeze to develop by 1400 or so, but the postwar building boom that turned Long Island's potato fields into housing developments, superhighways, and shopping centers has raised a barrier of heat that seems to have blocked the sea breeze until late in the afternoon. Sometimes it riffles in about 1700 and often it never makes it. Since the frequent calms are combined with a steady and all-pervasive bobble of powerboat wakes, the percentage of days with good sailing conditions is low.

All need not be lost, however. If the time can be arranged, a spring or fall cruise, mostly on weekdays in the eastern part of Long Island Sound, can still be rewarding. The breezes should be fresher and the harbors should not be so crowded. In the western sound, all-year home-base harbors such as City Island, Manhasset Bay, Larchmont, Mamaroneck, Greenwich, Stamford, Oyster Bay, Norwalk, and the rest are not likely targets for a cruising sailor. Huntington Bay's complex, base for a great many boats, does have some anchorages like Price's Bend that are pleasant when not too crowded, and on eastward from here an off-season cruise can be rewarding in such spots as the Norwalk Islands, Port Jefferson and its various arms, the Thimble Islands, Duck Island Roads, Mattituck, Fisher's Island, Mystic, and Stonington.

Around the tip of Long Island, between the "fishtail" in Gardiner's Bay and Peconic Bay, there are some delightful cruising harbors.

*Dering Harbor, Shelter Island, L.I.*

*Ducks flying over the Shrewsbury River.*

Shelter Island has several, Greenport is colorful, and Sag Harbor, Three Mile Harbor, and Montauk on the southern half of the fishtail all have something to offer. Montauk, of course, is a bustling sportfishing center, but the facilities and protection are good.

The answer to cruising on Long Island Sound is to pick your time of week and season to avoid the crowds, and the natural advantages can then be appreciated.

No one in his right mind would come to the New York area for a sailboat cruise, given all the excellent cruising areas there are not far from it, but those who base there, or transients with some time to explore a bit on their way through, might be surprised at the opportunities.

Manhattan itself is a wasteland for the yachtsman, although there have been recent stirrings toward adding new marinas to the two rather grubby ones that have been there for a while. Yachtsmen from overseas, coming into New York after a Transatlantic passage or a trip up the Waterway, are always shocked and amazed at the lack of facilities for

*A quiet corner of the Shrewsbury.*

yachts in a major seaport city when they are forced to berth on the far fringes of the metropolis, a disappointment after visions of stepping ashore to theaters, shops, and restaurants.

The fringes do, however, offer a chance for some offbeat cruising. First of all, City Island, at the western end of Long Island Sound, is within the city limits, and is a major boating center, with clubs, marinas, service yards, building yards, and restaurants, and a visitor can usually find a slip or a convenient spot to anchor. The East and Harlem Rivers that help to make Manhattan an island are commercial channels with heavy tides, to be negotiated through necessity only, not for pleasure, and the Hudson off Manhattan isn't much better, although the view of the skyscrapers and a Saturday afternoon glimpse of the parade of cruise liners leaving port can be enjoyable.

North of Manhattan, the Hudson has imposing scenery and a few places to stop along the Jersey shore and in the Nyack area. South from Manhattan, an enterprising skipper can find a place to anchor behind the Statue of Liberty if he is really looking for oddball adventure. The

*Islands and coves of the Shrewsbury.*

Brooklyn side of the harbor has Gravesend Bay, which has a couple of boatyards and is a fair-weather anchorage in anything but strong north-westers. The Lower Bay, which was the most active yachting area in the country in the mid-nineteenth century, provides a surprising number of anchorage opportunities, and an enterprising explorer could spend several days there. The breeze is usually excellent, and an afternoon excursion out past Ambrose Light Tower into the open Atlantic makes a delightful sail. In behind Coney Island, Sheepshead Bay is a bustling boating center in urban surroundings, and on through Rockaway Inlet, Jamaica Bay, surprisingly, offers some seclusion, especially on weekdays in an anchorage like Dead Horse Cove or amid the marshy islands in its center, where bird life abounds. Air traffic from Kennedy Airport also abounds here, which is something of a drawback.

On Staten Island, Great Kills Harbor has plenty of anchoring space and many yards and clubs, and across Raritan Bay, Keyport and Atlantic Highlands are sailing towns. The Municipal Marina at Atlantic Highlands is base for over four hundred boats, many of them fishing boats, but there is also a large fleet of cruising auxiliaries and plenty of anchoring space. Don't get caught here in a nor'easter, however. On the west side of Sandy Hook, the five-mile peninsula that juts north at the top end of the Jersey Coast, Horseshoe Cove is a popular overnight and luncheon stop in fair weather, and the shore is an unspoiled holly forest, set off by sand dunes, as part of a national park.

South of Sandy Hook, the Shrewsbury River system, twin tidal flats that cut into the pleasant hills of Monmouth County, has attractive shorelines, many marinas and waterfront restaurants, and a number of places to anchor in good protection and quiet surroundings.

The northern branch, leading to Red Bank, is called the Navesink, and the Shrewsbury itself parallels the narrow ocean beach running southward for several miles from Sandy Hook before becoming wider in a southwestward spread between Rumson and Oceanport. Monmouth Beach, at the southern terminus of the channel from Sandy Hook, has become a major yachting center. There is a great deal of local activity, but this is not an area known to cruising visitors. Someone with a few days to spare in the New York area might be agreeably surprised by the number of pleasant anchorages.

South of here, the Jersey Coast offers little in the way of cruising, although Barnegat Bay does have a number of coves and tributaries. It is reached through a tortuous river and canal system from Manasquan Inlet and is technically the start of the a section of the Intracoastal Waterway, but it has not been well maintained and controlling depths are minimum in many spots below Barnegat. Barnegat Inlet, incidentally, is one of the most treacherous on the coast and should not be used by strangers except in the direst emergency. Even local boats get in trouble on its shifting bars.

Absecon Inlet at Atlantic City and Cold Spring Inlet at Cape May are the only ones visitors should use in traversing the Jersey Coast. For boats with masts under 55 feet, the Cape May Canal is a shortcut to Delaware Bay and the route to the Chesapeake. Delaware Bay itself is the least attractive body of water on the Atlantic Coast from a cruising point of view, and the best advice on it is to get through it as quickly as possible, playing the tide if that can be arranged. It is strictly a utility route to the Chesapeake and points south.

# The Chesapeake Bay

| | |
|---|---|
| AREA: | 37° to 39° 40′ N   76°W |
| | 200 miles, north-south |
| SEASON: | April to mid-November |
| PREVAILING BREEZE: | Variable |
| CLIMATE: | Pleasantly warm in spring and fall, hot in summer |
| DRAFT LIMITS: | 4–6 feet for full cruising; above that, major harbors |
| TIDAL RANGE: | 1–3 feet |
| ANCHORAGES: | Unlimited |
| DRAWBACKS: | Heat, lack of wind, thunderstorms in midsummer; crowding in mid-bay area near Annapolis |
| PLUS FACTORS: | Unlimited choice of anchorages, creek gunkholing, attractive towns and villages, good fishing, crabbing |
| BOOKS: | *Waterway Guide* (annual, Mid-Atlantic edition); *Cruising Guide to Chesapeake Bay; Cruises Mainly in the Bay of the Chesapeake* |

The Chesapeake Bay is deservedly one of the most popular cruising grounds anywhere, as it provides more anchorages in a given area than any similar body of water. Even under the pressures of the boating boom and resultant overcrowding in recent years, it has so many creeks and byways, as well as populated boating centers with good facilities, that it is able to absorb a tremendous number of cruising boats. The mid-bay belt around Annapolis on the western shore and Oxford on the eastern shore has an enormous concentration of home-based boats, and a Sunday afternoon off Annapolis in early fall fills the bay with an incredible spread of sail. In the nearby harbors, such as Galesville and South River, as well as Annapolis itself, berthing space is hard to come by, and visitors must usually anchor out in a jammed harbor, but there are still a great many side creeks and small coves that provide a choice of cruising stops.

Even from Annapolis it is possible to head up the Severn River and find a measure of seclusion in some of its coves, and the South River has several tributary creeks that fulfill the same function. Nearby, the Rhode River can accommodate a big influx of visitors at anchor, and does every weekend; and the West River (which, illogically, is south of the South River), is crammed with marinas and restaurants catering to yachtsmen.

On the eastern shore, towns like Oxford and St. Michaels are home to large fleets of yachts but still manage to take on transients at their marinas and restaurant docks. Around them, on the Miles, Chester, and Choptank River systems, there is an amazing choice of secluded anchorages in tributary creeks and odd coves. While isolation is no longer guaranteed in any mid-Chesapeake anchorage, it is still possible to find peace and comparative privacy in many places.

Although the mid-bay area, with its proximity to Philadelphia, Baltimore, and Washington, sees the most activity, the Chesapeake has a great deal more to offer than this limited area in its two-hundred-mile length. In the north, Northeast, right at the head of the bay, and Georgetown, on the Sassafrass River, are popular bases because they are easily reached from Philadelphia, Wilmington, and other cities to the north, but they are rather far from the bay's main attractions. Weekending is confined to limited areas near home, like Worton Creek, and government reservations take up a big part of the western shore north of Baltimore.

South of the Choptank, the bay widens out and becomes less crowded, and the cruising sailor with some time to explore can poke into many an isolated backwater in rural peace and quiet. A list of the possible anchorages would run on for pages, and a study of local annual guides is recommended. Tangier and Smith Islands in the center of the bay are fascinating outposts, although they have recently been "discov-

*Crab Creek on the Chesapeake.*

*An arm of the Chesapeake's South River.*

ered" by a fairly steady tourist trade and have lost some of their old-world charm.

On the lower eastern shore, the Honga River and its tributaries remains relatively untouched, a land of low marshes and isolated villages where the life of the bay watermen who make their living by crabbing or oystering appears today as it has looked for generations. The lower Western shore is more civilized and developed, with such centers as Solomons and Deltaville crowded with boats, and a tremendous menhaden fishery with supporting shipyards has taken over Reedville on the Great Wicomico River.

The bigger tributary rivers, such as the Patuxent, Potomac, Rappahannock, York, and James, are cruising areas in themselves, with many side creeks and attractive towns, and one could spend the good part of a cruising lifetime just getting around to all the Mill Creeks there are in all parts of the Chesapeake. The Little Wicomico, the Piankatank, Mobjack Bay, and the Back River are smaller tributaries along the western shore, all worth poking into and in most cases still offering a measure of relief from overcrowding.

Crisfield on the eastern shore is a major seafood center and has good yacht facilities in a protected basin, and south of it the eastern shore is generally rural and undeveloped. The harbors are small, without many facilities, but still a lure for the adventurous.

Civilization closes in again with a vengeance in the Hampton Roads area at the foot of the bay. This is one of the best deep-water ports on the Atlantic Coast, a major naval base and a growing industrial area, with Norfolk as the center. A yacht moving through the busy channels of Hampton Roads seems somewhat overwhelmed and definitely dwarfed by the press of commercial and naval shipping. It is an interesting sight, though, to range along the navy piers and to thread through the ships at anchor and underway.

The yachtsman is far from ignored amid all this commercial atmosphere. Norfolk has an active yacht club with a pleasant marina and anchorage area, plus several marinas, and there is a big marina catering to transients in Portsmouth, across the harbor from Norfolk. This is the starting point of the Intracoastal Waterway to Florida, with a great flow of yacht traffic in spring and fall, and Norfolk, with good air transportation, is also a handy place to regroup forces, change crews, etc., while on a waterway passage.

The Chesapeake has all these physical advantages, and it would take a lifetime of cruising to sample all it has to offer, but it does have some physical disadvantages, or at least some characteristics that must be considered. The season is a long one, from April into November, and sometimes it can even be stretched at both ends with a bit of luck. However, it is not one long perfect season, as there are some drawbacks to Chesapeake cruising in the period from mid-June to mid-September. Although there is a prevailing afternoon breeze that blows up the bay from the south, it loses its punch in summer and there can be long periods of calm. Because it extends well inland, the Chesapeake is not under the influence of sea breezes except near its mouth, and it can be subject to heavy heat and humidity in summer, with calms as an adjunct. Heat waves also bring thunderstorms, and there is a high percentage of late-afternoon squalls in the same period. In some years the water is also infested with jellyfish, so there is no escape from the heat by diving into the water.

These factors vary by the year, and some summers are breezier and drier than others, but the chances are high for light winds, heat, and squalls in that three-month stretch. Conversely, in some winters the Chesapeake remains ice-free and some good sailing days can be seized even in January and February, but this is fairly rare. Then there was the winter of 1976–7 when the bay was frozen for almost two months.

The best times for Chesapeake cruising are early May to mid-June and mid-September into November, and these times coincide with the influx of transients heading south or north on the waterway, so many visitors do see it at its best time. There is also a growing trend toward chartering privately owned boats, and there are some commercially operated bareboat fleets, so there is little excuse for missing this prime cruising grounds.

# The Intracoastal Waterway: Norfolk to Key West

| | |
|---|---|
| AREA: | 36° 50' to 24° 33' N    76° 17' to 81° 48' W |
| | 1090 statute miles |
| SEASON: | Open all year: not recommended north of Georgia in January and February |
| PREVAILING BREEZE: | Varied |
| CLIMATE: | Normal seasonal changes; warmer in south |
| DRAFT LIMITS: | Over 8 feet can cause problems in spots (mast height limit 65 feet) |
| TIDAL RANGE: | Varies by area but not a big factor |
| NUMBER OF ANCHORAGES: | Unlimited |
| DRAWBACKS: | Monotony in a few stretches, powerboat and barge traffic, northern half poor in winter |
| PLUS FACTORS: | Interesting towns and many scenic stretches, good protection in most areas, good facilities |
| BOOKS: | *Waterway Guide* (annual, Mid-Atlantic and Southern editions); *Cruising Guide to the Southern Coast; The Boy, Me and the Cat; The Inside Passage* |

The Intracoastal Waterway is more than just a ditch. It is, in truth, extremely varied over its full length, which technically goes from New England to Texas, but the main portion of it, as dealt with here, is the 1090 statute miles—the units by which it is marked and charted—from Norfolk, Virginia, to Miami. To many who travel it, the ICW is just a highway south, a means of getting a boat to southern waters in the fall and back north in the spring, and they look on it with all the warmth and affection they lavish on Route I-95.

There are others, though, to whom the waterway is a true and very satisfying cruising experience, and I number myself among them. In a sailboat there are long periods under power. In fact there are only a few sections where one can count on having a sail, even when time is not a factor, and yet the pace of a cruising auxiliary seems to make an ICW trip a more relaxed one than the hurry-on-by tempo of a powerboat. Then, when the chance does come to put up the sails, there is an extra feeling of excitement and release in being under sail again after all that powering.

The best way to take the waterway, therefore, is as a cruise rather than a ferry trip, and it then becomes a much more satisfying experience. If one has the time to walk around an interesting town, to poke up a side creek into the pine forests, to sightsee the old houses of Charleston, South Carolina, or to run down the Alligator River under sail, the rewards are multiple. You're getting somewhere, but you are having a good time while you're at it.

In traveling the waterway, it is important to have the latest edition of the *Waterway Guide* annual in hand, as there are changes every year in the facilities that are offered at certain places (new ones opening up or old ones going out of business), and in new bridges or other physical features. Even on an annual basis the *Guide* can become outdated, as we found out once in poking into a harbor after dark and tying up at a marina pier. We hit the sack immediately without checking around, and it was a surprise in the morning to find no trace of the marina described in the *Guide* except for its pier. The place had burned to the ground six months earlier and there wasn't a sign left of its buildings.

The ads in the *Guide* are helpful, but sometimes they must be taken with a grain of salt as to the actual existence of facilities offered, and even in the controlling draft quoted. Also, restaurants are sometimes just snackbars or have gone out of business, but these are minor matters. It is the height of foolhardiness to take the ICW trip without the *Guide*.

One thing to remember in a relatively slow auxiliary is that the day's runs can be quite different between spring and fall. In October

*A busy marina at Portsmouth, Virginia, at the start of the ICW.*

and November, when most boats are on their way down, the days are very short and a little over ten hours is the best you can get of daylight. In the spring this expands to as much as fourteen hours and much longer runs are possible. The waterway can be negotiated at night if you really want to work hard, but it's much better to stick to daylight running.

It is possible to make a marina almost every night if you want the amenities of shore power, shopping, and eating ashore, but it is also possible to anchor almost every night and reduce the ever-increasing dockage fees. There are long stretches of canal where it is impossible to anchor, but careful planning can time your runs to end at dark in an area of side creeks or coves. If you do plan to anchor a lot, many of the anchorages are in marshy areas, and it's important to have your boat well screened. A spot that seems bug free when a breeze is blowing can suddenly buzz to life with mosquitos after the breeze dies.

Most marinas are hospitable to auxiliaries despite their low fuel demands, although there are some that hold their transient berths for big powerboats until just about dark. When fuel availability is a problem, powerboat owners often reserve ahead at marinas where they are known, but it is an exception to have a marina discriminate against sailboats. One big marina at Portsmouth, Virginia, at the start of the ICW, which gets a great bulk of the total traffic in and out of its fuel dock and slips, has a section of the fuel dock marked off for sailboats, which seems to make sense. Space is left open for the fuel guzzlers, but sailboats are obviously welcome and catered to.

Mile Zero for the Norfolk-Miami section of the ICW is off the big naval hospital in Portsmouth and right near the marina mentioned above. North of there, the waterway is not specially marked, and even though you are on the prescribed route you are just in the Chesapeake, Long Island Sound, or whatever. From Norfolk south the special waterway markers are used, with even-numbered orangy-red triangles to starboard and odd-numbered bright-green squares to port when heading south. In many places there are five-mile markers, with statute miles used, as I have mentioned. In general, the channel markers are well placed and easy to follow as long as you don't lose track. Sometimes a section of the ICW will be part of a channel that is regularly marked with "red-right-returning" in from the sea in opposition to waterway numbering, and a careful check must be kept in these areas.

I have often been asked about alternating sections of the ICW with offshore passages between inlets. This is possible in fast power-boats, but there are very few sections in which a sailboat can duck out an inlet in the morning and come back in again at night after a reasonable day's run offshore. Most of the usable inlets are far enough apart to require overnight passages, which means watchstanding and a bigger crew, so you would have to be set up for this kind of operation in advance.

The ICW controling bridge height is 65 feet, although boats with taller sticks can go inside from Norfolk to Morehead City, North Carolina, avoiding the passage around Cape Hatteras, by taking a circuitous route through drawbridges to bypass a fixed bridge near Morehead. Also, a bridge near Norfolk requires 24-hour advance notice before opening for boats with masts taller than 65 feet. The outside route around Hatteras should be avoided in all cases, unless the boat is set up for a nonstop offshore passage all the way from the north to Florida or vice versa, a far different project from taking the ICW.

One of the joys of a waterway trip is the "fellowship of the road." Especially in auxiliaries, which have similar cruising speeds and tend to make about the same day's runs, there is a tendency to meet with the same boats repeatedly, and a camaraderie of shared experience springs up rapidly. Yesterday's stranger is tonight's long-lost friend when you end up in the same marina, and the visiting back and forth, mutual help, and comparing of notes enhance the whole experience very pleasantly. Some owners have made the passage year after year and know all the tricks and angles, and their advice can be very helpful.

We have also found that 99 percent of the powerboat people passing us are thoughtful and courteous, slowing down to reduce wake as they move by, and we always give them a grateful wave. It is really rare to have a hot-shot cowboy charge on by without so much as one rpm off the throttle or a sideways glance as his wake bounces you around and smashes against the banks of the waterway, but there still are a few.

A waterway trip is a form of nautical nature walk and as such can

*Virginia Cut on the Intracoastal Waterway.*

provide great enjoyment. There are, to be sure, some rather arid stretches between canal banks when there isn't much to look at, such as the twenty-six-mile canal back of Myrtle Beach, South Carolina, where the only excitement is to see the aerial tramway cars carrying golfers from one hole to another over your head. For the most part, though, there is something new to see around each bend, and even some of the other canals, like the Virginia Cut or the Alligator-Pungo, offer views of foliage, wildlife, and an occasional farm or small town.

The North Carolina Sounds have an awful lot of water, and there are sections of the waterway, such as crossing Albemarle Sound, where you are almost out of sight of land, and quite a chop can kick up when the wind blows. We have had some exciting slides across it in fresh fall northwesters. The Neuse River is another wide-open stretch where, looking to the eastward, the horizon is completely empty as the Outer Banks are far beyond the limits of visibility. Maw Point, where Pamlico Sound and the Neuse River come together, is one of the notorious rough spots of the ICW, and many a small boat has taken a real beating rounding it in a nor'easter.

Anyone with the time to spare can linger in these North Carolina waters for some side cruising that is very pleasant. Here there is no question of overcrowding, and there are any number of quiet anchorages in the waters off the main ICW route. The Outer Banks are a fascinating world apart and well worth a visit, although draft must be watched in getting out to them through a maze of sandbars in Pamlico Sound. The Neuse River, with its side creeks, is a fine cruising ground, and one of its tributaries, Adams Creek, has a number of delightful gunkholes and is one of the prettiest areas on the entire ICW. On a late March cruise out of Oriental, North Carolina, on the Neuse, an active center for several hundred auxiliaries, we ventured out Beaufort Inlet at Morehead City to Cape Lookout, and had the enormous bight inside the barrier beach there—big enough to hold every sailboat in North Carolina and then some—completely to ourselves in weather like a summer day in New England. In some mild winters, sailing is possible on good days right through the year, and the season stretches from March to December in any event. Summers are hot and tend to light air, but out near the ocean on the banks, sea breezes keep things cooler and provide good sailing all through the summer. As in the Chesapeake, afternoon squalls are a factor, but not quite as frequently.

South of Morehead City, which is a bustling port for yachts, fishing boats, and commercial shipping, the character of the ICW changes somewhat. Morehead is a favorite jumping-off port for boats bound offshore to the Caribbean, especially in the fall, and fast power-boats and larger sailboats often head outside from here on their way to Florida after avoiding the Hatteras menace. There are no more really big bodies of water like Albemarle and Pamlico Sounds, and there is more "ditch-crawling." Much of this is fascinating, though, with wild-life sanctuaries, quaint old towns, summer colonies on the barrier beaches, and changing vegetation to look for. Moss appears on the trees and palmettos are part of the scene. Egrets, seen all along the ICW, become even more numerous, poised against the banks or flapping lazily overhead, and on some low trees near Morehead where they roost they look as though a great deal of laundry had been spread out to dry.

There are some relatively dull stretches, and some real beauty, as on South Carolina's Waccamaw River, winding through great moss-hung forests. South of Charleston there are more "ditches" but also some lovely stretches back of the sea islands of South Carolina and Georgia, and from Jacksonville's urban sprawl onward one is in the semitropical atmosphere of Florida.

A nautical I-95 it might be for some, but for those who can take the time to appreciate it, the Intracoastal Waterway makes a wonderful, and quite different, kind of cruising.

# The Great Lakes

| AREA: | 41° 10′ to 49° N     76° to 92° W |
|---|---|
| | 480 by 700 miles |
| SEASON: | June through September |
| PREVAILING BREEZE: | Southwest |
| CLIMATE: | Cool north, warm south; some summer heat waves |
| DRAFT LIMITS: | Not a factor |
| TIDAL RANGE: | None, but water levels change by the year, and in wind tides called seiches |
| NUMBER OF ANCHORAGES: | Unlimited |
| DRAWBACKS: | Short season, summer thunder squalls, long stretches of open water, limited facilities near cities |
| PLUS FACTORS: | Many interesting areas and good scenery, good fishing and swimming, wide choice of areas |

One look at a map and it is obvious that cruising opportunities abound in the Great Lakes. From the upper end of the St. Lawrence to the western end of Lake Superior, this vast complex has to be a natural for the cruising sailor. Aside from the tremendous spread of square miles of water, there are special extras the coastal sailor misses, like no tide rise or fall and no current, and all the fresh water you can drink, wash in, and wash down with.

There is great variety on the lakes. Some shorelines, like much of Lakes Ontario, Erie, and Michigan, are unbroken for many miles, with only a few man-made harbors to break the monotony, while other areas, like the North Channel and Georgian Bay off Lake Huron, the Bay of

*Morning calm along Chicago's lakefront.*

Quinte in Lake Ontario, Green Bay and Door County on Lake Michigan, and much of Lake Superior, are rich in islands, coves, side channels, and natural harbors.

The big cities like Buffalo, Toronto, Cleveland, Detroit, Chicago, and Milwaukee are naturally home base for a great many boats, but all of them are fairly well removed from the best cruising areas. Locally based boats take part in many day and overnight races, weekend to one nearby harbor, or just go out and come back, but almost everyone saves up time for a vacation cruise to Georgian Bay or one of the other popular escape areas.

Since the season is very short, activity is frantic while the weather is good. Much of it is crammed into July and August, although June and September can be good months in all but the more northern areas. Summer has its problems too, with a fairly high percentage of light air and the ever-present threat of thunder squalls. When a heat wave from the great plains spreads its smothering blanket over the lakes, conditions are not the greatest for sailing.

In the prime cruising areas, particularly Georgian Bay and the North Channel, the atmosphere is very reminiscent of Maine, with pine-topped, rocky shores and a zestful clarity to the atmosphere, a real north woods tang, when the weather is right. Like the Maine Coast, this area is also shot through with channels, passages, and thoroughfares that wind between islands and around headlands, and there is an unlimited number of anchorages to choose from, as well as a few cruising centers where boats gather for supplies, such as Little Current and Thessalon. Although just about every cruising boat in the lakes heads for this area during July and August, there are so many little hideaways with good cruising anchorages that it is still possible to get away from it all for at least part of the time.

From Lake Ontario, it is a long way up to Huron, and many local boats are content with the Bay of Quinte and the area around the western end of the St. Lawrence River, where it begins its long journey to the sea by threading through the Thousand Islands. These live up to their name in offering anchorages, and the peaceful, bucolic surroundings of the Bay of Quinte on the Canadian side of the lake make a very pleasant cruising area. On the New York side, Chaumont, Henderson Harbor, and the surroundings bays and islands are a little world apart.

From the eastern end of Lake Erie, cruising people without the extra time needed to get through Detroit and Lake St. Clair to the prime areas on Huron often settle for a few days in the Lake Erie islands. These are the remnants of an old land bridge across the lake from the Sandusky area to Canada. Put-in-Bay is the yachting hub of this region, with the fluted tower of the Perry Monument, commemorating the Battle of Lake Erie in 1813, dominating the scene.

Chicagoans who don't have the time to push on through the Straits of Mackinac to the North Channel area can spend a pleasant few days in Green Bay, Wisconsin, and the Door County Peninsula

*The North Channel of Lake Huron near Desbarats.*

that separates Green Bay from the main lake; and the Beaver Islands, out in the center of the northern end of the lake, have a few good harbors amid unspoiled surroundings.

The local population of boats on Lake Superior is relatively small, and it is also a long push for boats from the other lakes, but the clear waters, bracing air, and rugged wilderness areas of much of its shoreline are a real challenge to experienced cruising sailors. A special feature here is Isle Royale, a large, isolated, relatively untouched island in the western end of the lake. A cruising boat in Lake Superior is on its own for days at a time, very often without seeing another boat, and a wise skipper keeps a constant eye on the weather, as it can make up rapidly, with impressive effect, on this biggest of all the Great Lakes.

# The Florida Keys and West Coast

| | |
|---|---|
| AREA: | 24° 33' to 28° N    80° 05' to 82° 50' W |
| | 200 by 90 miles |
| SEASON: | All year |
| PREVAILING BREEZE: | South to southeast |
| CLIMATE: | Very warm in summer, some winter cold snaps |
| DRAFT LIMITS: | Over 6 feet a problem |
| TIDAL RANGE: | 1–3 feet |
| NUMBER OF ANCHORAGES: | Unlimited |
| DRAWBACKS: | Many shoal areas, winter northers, summer thunderstorms |
| PLUS FACTORS: | Long season; good fishing, swimming, diving; good facilities; interesting ports |
| BOOKS: | *Waterway Guide* (annual, Southern edition); *Cruising Guide to the Southern Coast; Cruising Guide to the Florida Keys* |

The east coast of Florida is virtually one long, straight beach, with the Intracoastal Waterway behind it, and it is not an attractive area for the cruising sailor. Once on it, the skipper interested in good cruising waters should just keep moving until he gets to Miami, where a significant change in the lay of the land opens up some good cruising waters in the Keys and all the way around the west coast of Florida to just north of Tampa Bay.

Although there are seasonal problems in both winter and summer, this is in truth an all-year area, which is an immediate plus, and the delights of subtropical surroundings are another. The water is clear and warm, the swimming and diving are good, as is the fishing, and the choice of harbors is wide. The good cruising area starts right at Miami,

*Cruising the Gulf of Mexico.*

with Biscayne Bay a wonderful "safety valve" for the thousands of boats that base there. Separating Miami from Miami Beach at its northern end, where it is full of man-made islands and causeways, it is almost smothered by civilization's advances, but south of the Rickenbacker Causeway, which connects Key Biscayne with the mainland, Biscayne Bay is a delightful sailing area, stretching south for about thirty miles into the Keys, and up to ten miles wide at some points. The breeze is usually good, and there is plenty of water for hoisting the sails and letting her go. Weekending can be done at Elliott Key or Key Largo's many harbors, and longer cruises can take in an almost infinite succession of harbors all the way to Key West, one hundred forty miles away at the end of the line. The Marquesas and Dry Tortugas, out in the Gulf of Mexico beyond Key West, are home-grown "South Sea islands," exciting, far-away places to visit.

The Keys are not ideal for sailing, since the water is pretty thin in many places, and it is necessary to stick to the winding ICW channel. A shoal-draft boat (under 4 feet) can ignore this in many areas, and bigger boats can take the outside route in the Hawk Channel on the seaward side of the Keys, or even poke on out through the many cuts in the barrier reef and sail in the Gulf Stream. There are marinas galore, and spots like Jewfish Creek, Tavernier, Islamorada, and Marathon are particularly busy with sportfishing boats, although sailboats can be accommodated in most spots. Leisurely gunkholing in a shallow-draft boat, preferably a centerboarder, would be the best kind of sailboat cruising in the Keys.

Between the Keys and the southernmost tip of the Florida mainland is a broad, shallow body of water called Florida Bay, and once across it via a marked channel known as the Yacht Channel, a cruising sailboat is in more rewarding waters. There are a few cays in Florida Bay that can be used as a lee for overnight anchoring, and there are a couple of creeks near Cape Sable, the southern tip of the mainland, that can be ducked into if you have screens and insect repellent, but it isn't until Naples, a day's run up the west coast from Cape Sable, that the good cruising country really begins. Another problem in Florida Bay and the Cape Sable area is a profusion of lobster pots in the water that make night running virtually impossible.

Naples is an attractive, well-heeled community with a good harbor and yacht facilities, but there is a dead spot in the ICW from there north for thirty miles to the Fort Myers area, an easy day's run in the gulf. Then Pine Island Sound and Charlotte Harbor, separated from the gulf by Sanibel, Captiva, and Gasparilla Islands, famous for shell collecting, contain all sorts of anchorages, well worth a cruise of a week or so right here.

The ICW is easily negotiable from here to Tampa Bay via Venice and Sarasota, or one can choose to make passages in the gulf, with a good choice of inlets, or passes as they are known here, for popping in and out. Tampa Bay is a large body of water with heavy commercial traffic and a tremendous concentration of yachts, and a week can be profitably spent sampling its many anchorages, from the Manatee River in the south to Clearwater in the north, and on to the isolated, attractive Anclote Keys off Tarpon Springs. St. Petersburg is one of the major yachting capitals of the country, with every facility imaginable, and there is plenty of room to sail on Tampa Bay's broad expanse, or out in the gulf itself.

Although this is an all-year area, there are seasonal changes. In the winter, northers blast in with cold air from the midwest, dropping the temperature to near freezing several times a winter, and in summer the west coast of Florida, shut off from the cooling "trade wind" southeaster of the east coast, suffers from light air and a heavy concentration of thunderstorms. Skipping around these inconveniences, there is still a high percentage of days in a calendar year when it is pleasant to be cruising under sail here.

# The Channel Islands

| | |
|---|---|
| AREA: | 33° to 34°N   118° 15′ to 120° 30′ W |
| | 60 by 110 miles |
| SEASON: | Year round, but summer is better |
| PREVAILING BREEZE: | Westerly |
| CLIMATE: | Pleasantly cool to warm |
| DRAFT LIMITS: | Not a factor |
| TIDAL RANGE: | 6–7 feet |
| NUMBER OF ANCHORAGES: | Fewer than three dozen |
| DRAWBACKS: | Winter fogs, Santana storms (east wind from the desert), lack of facilities, private control of islands |
| PLUS FACTORS: | Long season; good swimming, fishing, diving; generally good climate |
| BOOKS: | *Sea Boating Almanac* (annual, Southern California edition); *Cruising the Pacific Coast; Cruising Guide to the Channel Islands* |

Californians are very limited in their cruising opportunities. The heavily populated harbors of the stretch of coast between Santa Barbara and San Diego give on a relatively empty ocean, and cruising along the coast from harbor to harbor is an unrewarding prospect. The harbors are jammed full of locally based boats, and a visitor on a cruise cannot just pop in and drop the hook or pick up a slip for a night or two, as is common practice on the East Coast. Advance reservations must be made, if there are any openings at all, and it is a very formalized, regimented type of operation.

Unless one takes off for Mexico, which means a cruise of at least

*Off-season in a Catalina Island cove. In summer the buoys would all be occupied.*

a couple of months if not more, the only way to cruise in Southern California is to head to the few islands that lie offshore. The major one is Catalina, twenty-five miles away across the Catalina Channel, and such are the pressures on it as a target for weekending and cruising that its many coves, mostly on the north shore facing the mainland, are controlled by clubs or organizations, who have placed mooring buoys in them and administer the use of the buoys, or contain moorings that are leased out to individual owners by the season. The whole island is privately owned and controlled by a corporation. Unless you go over there in the middle of the week in the winter, you have to make arrangements for where you are going to moor.

A weekend in a Catalina cove has all the privacy of Dodger Stadium during the World Series, but at least it's a place to head for from the mainland. The other islands in this offshore group known as the Channel Islands are beautiful physically but do not have many harbors, and they too are under private or governmental control, so that there is no such thing as casual dropping in here.

There is the advantage of a virtual year-round season for those who are fanatics, although activity is minimal during midwinter. While the climate is generally mild, fogs are a real problem in winter and spring, and another real hazard is the hot, dry, desert wind known as a Santana. Under certain conditions, this takes over from the prevailing sea breeze westerlies and sends a furnace blast of wind of up to 50 knots out from shore to raise hell in the north-shore coves of Catalina, which then become completely exposed. The only harbor on Catalina with all-directions protection is on the south or seaward side at the Isthmus, where the mountainous, twenty-two-mile island narrows down at its center to a low strip only a few hundred yards across.

Despite these drawbacks, a tremendous number of cruising auxiliaries operate out of Southern California ports.

*Tinsley Island station of St. Francis Y.C. in the Sacramento Delta.*

# The Sacramento River Delta

| | |
|---|---|
| AREA: | 38° to 38° 20′ N    121° 40′ to 122° 15′ W |
| | 20 by 40 miles |
| SEASON: | Year round, but summer is very hot |
| PREVAILING BREEZE: | Westerly |
| CLIMATE: | Cool to very hot |
| DRAFT LIMITS: | Unlimited, but larger boats with a shallow draft have more opportunities |
| TIDAL RANGE: | 3 feet, but floods occur |
| NUMBER OF ANCHORAGES: | Unlimited |
| DRAWBACKS: | Completely inland, not much sailing, heat waves, floods |
| PLUS FACTORS: | Picturesque gunkholing, hundreds of miles of waterway |
| BOOKS: | *Sea Boating Almanac* (annual, Northern California edition); *Cruising the Pacific Coast* |

The San Francisco Bay area provides no offshore cruising grounds to head for. Beyond the rocky pinnacles of the Farallons outside the Golden Gate, which have no harbor, there is just the broad, open Pacific all the way to Hawaii. Instead, bay sailors have to look inland for a cruising escape, and they have it in the Sacramento River Delta area that extends well inland from the head of the bay.

This is not the kind of place you go for exciting passages under sail, as it is all inland once you leave the bay itself, with hundreds of miles of waterways (known as sloughs) winding through the flat, marshy delta country. When the wind is fair, it is possible to hoist sails and slide between the tules (the high reeds that line the marshes) in a rural

*Looking across the Golden Gate at San Francisco from Tiburon.*

dreamland, but there is no room to work to windward anywhere in the delta in a good-size cruising boat.

The advantage is in a complete escape from civilized surroundings to picturesque gunkholing in complete isolation, or to the few backwater communities on pilings that are found occasionally throughout the area. There is an unending choice of anchorages, as it is possible to poke the bow into the bank and just stay there almost anywhere; there are a few marinas, or at least settlements with some pilings or a bulkhead where it is possible to tie up. St. Francis Yacht Club maintains a station at Tinsley Island, an abandoned lighthouse a day's run upriver from San Francisco, and many bay boats make this a target for a cruise.

Although year-round operations are possible it can get extremely hot in the delta in summer, but it's the best way to get away from it all that San Francisco cruising sailors have.

*Cruising the delta.*

# Puget Sound and the San Juans

| AREA: | 47° to 49° N     122° 10′ to 123° 30′ W |
| --- | --- |
| | 120 by 50 miles |
| SEASON: | Year round, but summer is better |
| PREVAILING BREEZE: | Variable, with westerlies most likely |
| CLIMATE: | Cool and wet |
| DRAFT LIMITS: | Not a factor |
| TIDAL RANGE: | 6–10 feet |
| NUMBER OF ANCHORAGES: | Unlimited |
| DRAWBACKS: | Wet weather, much fog and rain, strong currents in many areas, cold water |
| PLUS FACTORS: | Scenery, choice of harbors, long season, fishing |
| BOOKS: | *Sea Boating Almanac* (Pacific Northwest edition); *Cruising the Pacific Coast* |

One of the greatest concentrations anywhere of cruising boats per capita is in Puget Sound, and a look at the chart shows the reason why. The sound and the waters to the north of it in British Columbia, including Vancouver Island, offer an endless number of harbors in the most attractive kind of north woods setting, a long season that some hardy souls keep going for twelve months, and some of the most magnificent background scenery anywhere in the world.

Right from the south end of Puget Sound, where Mt. Rainier's majestic, snow-capped bulk looms over Tacoma and Commencement Bay, to the Straits of Juan de Fuca, the corridor between Puget Sound and the Pacific, wooded foreshores are backed by mountain ranges. On the Olympic Peninsula, which separates Puget Sound from the Pacific, the Olympic chain, usually capped by snow on its higher slopes, is a dramatic array of jagged peaks, with Mount Olympus the highest at

*A typical log boom tow on Puget Sound.*

7900 feet. Inland from the northeastern part of the sound, Mount Baker's Snowy, symmetrical, ten-thousand-foot dome looms on the far horizon like a distant cloud.

The word "sound" conjures images of an open stretch of water that is well landlocked, but Puget Sound is so landlocked and so island-filled that there are very few areas where there is a real open expanse. It is at its broadest just inside Juan de Fuca, but there are always nearby islands and the mainland in view, and one never loses sight of the mountains, at least when the visibility is good. Rain and fog are an integral part of the maritime climate here.

The best section for cruising in the Puget Sound area is in the San Juan Islands. These lie between Vancouver Island, which forms the north side of Juan de Fuca, and the mainland, right at the U.S.-Canadian border. In a caprice of local weather systems, they are noted for having sunnier weather than any other part of the Pacific Northwest, as the oceanic weather coming in through Juan de Fuca seems to split and go up or down the sound once it passes the Olympics on the south and the bulk of Vancouver Island to the north. This leaves

233

*Roche Harbor in the San Juan Islands.*

an open area in between, with the San Juans in it, and they are known locally as the "sunny San Juans."

They are a day's run from Seattle, or perhaps a two-day one for the leisurely auxiliary skipper, and a lot depends on the tides since these run very strongly in the passes between the islands. In Deception Pass, leading to the San Juans, the current, complete with giant eddies and whirlpools, can run up to 6 knots, and many an auxiliary has to plan things carefully to get through here.

Harbors abound and a choice can be made between isolation and crowded conviviality, since there are so many. West Sound on Orcas Island is a fine harbor, and Roche Harbor in San Juan Island is one of the busiest centers, with a large marina and a shoreside hotel. Across the border in Canada, the Pender Islands also have many places to stop, and when we were there the Customs formalities coming and going between the two countries were quickly accomplished.

Vancouver Island is a separate world, and its western side, giving on the open Pacific, is a relatively untouched wilderness with many fine harbors. Operating here is a real challenge in the tides, fogs, and weather vagaries of an isolated area. The city of Victoria has an excellent harbor and an old-world atmosphere that provides a real sense of being "abroad."

With all the choices there are of fine harbors to poke into and scenery to enjoy, there is also the plus of a long season. The winters tend to be mild, if a bit damp, and many owners never take their boats out of commission. From a sailing point of view, there is a drawback in that the average wind strength is quite light, especially around Seattle in the summer. In fact, conditions tend to be calm so often then that most local club racing is suspended, and everyone takes off to the northward for a cruising interlude.

*Marinas in Nassau, Bahamas.*

# The Bahamas, Turks, and Caicos

| | |
|---|---|
| AREA: | 21° to 27° 30′ N      71° to 79° 30′ W |
| | 390 by 480 miles, 600 on the bias |
| SEASON: | Year round |
| PREVAILING BREEZE: | Southeast and northeast |
| CLIMATE: | Subtropical to tropical |
| DRAFT LIMITS: | 6 feet, for all practical purposes |
| TIDAL RANGE: | 3–5 feet |
| NUMBER OF ANCHORAGES: | Unlimited |
| DRAWBACKS: | Winter northers, fall hurricanes, shallow water |
| PLUS FACTORS: | Climate, good breezes, fishing, snorkeling, swimming, long season, choice of harbors, water colors |
| BOOKS: | *Yachtsman's Guide to the Bahamas* (annual); *Waterway Guide* (annual; Southern edition); *The Bahamas; A Cruising Guide to the Caribbean and Bahamas* |

American cruising sailors are very lucky to have one of the world's premium cruising areas so near to home shores. The Bahamas are accessible for owners who take the time to get their own boats there, which more and more are doing every year, and there are chartering opportunities as well.

This is a vast area covering thousands of square miles in the Atlantic from fifty miles off the Florida coast to one hundred miles from the island of Hispaniola in the Greater Antilles. The Bahamas are not the Caribbean, as so many advertising copywriters will have you believe. They are in the Atlantic, and if they were not there—a great submerged plateau with a few areas sticking above the surface—the

*The Saddle Cay anchorage in the Exumas.*

climate of the northeastern United States and of northern Europe would be bleakly arctic in nature and virtually unlivable. It is this mighty barrier formed by the Bahama Banks that funnels the Gulf Stream into its concentrated path northeastward as the dominant controlling factor in the climate of the whole North Atlantic basin.

This big barrier, with its bits of islands here and there on a great expanse of warm shallow water, makes an ideal cruising grounds physically, and the climate also allows year-round operations, with an eye out for winter northers and autumn hurricanes. It would take a steady application to cruising over many years to take in all the places there are to explore in the Bahamas, although the bulk of the cruising traffic is concentrated in the central islands, with the capital city of Nassau on New Providence as the hub, one hundred sixty miles east of Miami.

We have taken our own three cruising boats to the Bahamas a total of five times so far, and it was well worth the effort to do it. We intend to get back there as often as possible, because there is still a great deal more to do and see, and we also enjoy returning often to favorite places.

*Compass Cay, Exumas.*

*Staniel Cay, Exumas.*

Getting there in most cases means crossing the Gulf Stream from Florida, and this is not a passage to be taken lightly. I have made the crossing over two dozen times, counting Southern Ocean Racing Conference races, cruises, and subchaser operations in World War II, and I always face the prospect with some anxiety. There have been crossings of millpond serenity (rare), some that were just good sails, and quite a few that were tough going. The best general advice is to try to pick your weather and then get there as fast as possible. Usually in an auxiliary this means motor-sailing, as a slow passage in the swift northward current of the stream, which can run at 2.5–3 knots on occasion, presents difficulties in making a desired landfall. If at all possible, crossing in a norther, with the wind against the current kicking up a wicked sea, should be avoided. Crossing the vast shallow Great Bahama Bank, a fifty-mile run east from Bimini and Cat Cay, is a unique experience.

Of all the areas to cruise in the Bahamas, with the Abacos, Berry Islands, Eleuthera, Exumas, southern Out Islands, and Turks and

Caicos group as the main divisions, I would choose the Exumas as the best, which is not to say that the others are not good. The Exumas, a closely knit hundred-mile chain of small cays running southeastward from a point thirty miles from Nassau, offer some of the most gorgeous water colors and perfect sailing in good breezes and smooth water to be found anywhere. There are harbors and gunkholes galore, and the northern half, from Staniel Cay north, usually has many more boats than the southern stretch from Staniel to George Town. It would be impossible to list all the lovely stops, but among my top favorites are Warderick Wells North, Shroud Cay, and the Pipe Creek area just north of Staniel, and Darby Island and Stocking Island in the southern sector.

To get away from other boats and experience Out Island life at its most natural, it's a good idea to head out to remoter islands like Long Island, Cat Island, Crooked Island, and Mayaguana, and the Turks and Caicos group is the ultimate in far out. They are politically a British colony but physically a part of the Bahamas, and a good week or two could well be spent gunkholing around the big Caicos Bank, which is ringed by the islands of the group.

Eleuthera, a day's run east of Nassau, has many good harbors, most rather well developed and civilized, and Spanish Wells, just off the northern tip, is a unique community whose lifestyle goes back to Revolutionary times, altered now by prosperity from lobster fishing.

North of Nassau, the Berry Islands are a compact group with several delightful harbors, not particularly crowded. It is a whole separate world in the Little Bahama Bank and the Abacos, which have some of the best protected waters for cruising inside the fringing reef, and some fascinating communities to visit, such as Hope Town and Man o' War, similar to Spanish Wells in carrying on a largely departed way of life.

If you only have time to get to Bimini and Cat Cay, directly across the Gulf Stream from Miami, there is still the thrill of "going foreign" and some authentic Bahamian atmosphere, somewhat colored by proximity to Florida. This is where the best sportfishing is, right on the edge of the Gulf Stream.

Anyone who cruises here has to use the *Yachtsman's Guide,* an

*Hopetown in the Abacos.*

absolute must for navigation in the absence of good charts, and for keeping up with annual changes in facilities and laws. It gives full information on entry procedures and other requirements (you can't stay longer than six months without paying duty on your boat), on Bahamian life and customs, on weather patterns, and everything else you need to know.

Because of Bahamian regulations, there are very few crewed charter boats operating there, but bareboats are available out of Nassau and the Abacos.

# The Virgin Islands (including St. Croix) and Vieques Sound

| | |
|---|---|
| AREA: | 17° 40' to 18° 40' N    64° 20' to 65° 30' W<br>60 by 80 miles |
| SEASON: | Year round, autumn not as desirable |
| PREVAILING BREEZE: | Northeast to southeast |
| CLIMATE: | Tropical |
| DRAFT LIMITS | Not a factor |
| TIDE RANGE: | 2 feet |
| NUMBER OF<br>    ANCHORAGES: | Unlimited |
| DRAWBACKS: | Strong midwinter winds, hurricanes |
| PLUS FACTORS: | Climate, good breezes, choice of harbors, fishing, swimming, diving, easy navigation |
| BOOKS: | *Yachtsman's Guide to the Greater Antilles and Virgin Islands* (annual); *The Virgin Islands; Street's Cruising Guide to the Eastern Caribbean* (vol. II); *West from the Virgins* |

The Virgin Islands have become the charter-boat capital of the world. From a modest start in the mid-1960s, there are now over three hundred bareboats for charter there, plus a professionally crewed fleet of over one hundred bigger yachts. The two main centers are Charlotte Amalie on St. Thomas in the American Virgins, and Road Town, Tortola, in the British Virgins. Even though the whole chain is only about fifty miles long and ten miles wide (not counting the American island of St. Croix, thirty-five miles off to the south by itself) it is split politically between the British and American groups, with the dividing line between St. John and Tortola, and yachts passing between the two political groups must go through Customs formalities.

This compactness is part of the charm of the Virgins, although it is now also a part of a growing problem of overcrowding as the charter fleets proliferate. There are so many harbors to choose from that there is no place in the islands where you are more than three miles away from a good anchorage, and this makes for the easiest kind of relaxed cruising. It is possible to make a leisurely morning start, stop for a swim and lunch or some diving, and sail on to another stop in the afternoon, repeating the pattern every day for a cruise of up to two weeks without running out of harbors.

The winds, almost always from the east, are about as reliable as in any cruising area in the world, somewhat light and fitful in the fall and tending to the boisterous in midwinter; the sun shines as much as it does anywhere else; and there are no major hazards in the way of open-water passages, notorious rough spots, or tricky navigation. Careful eyeballing in daytime should avoid what reefs there are, although there are always some people who don't manage to.

There is great diving for the casual and the serious, and the swimming and fishing are naturally fine too. In many of the harbors there are Out Island–type resorts or picturesque native restaurants for eating ashore, and for those who want it, Charlotte Amalie is a duty-free shopping heaven, with the resultant crowds of tourists from hotels and cruise ships.

There is no time that is a bad time to cruise in the Virgins, except perhaps the hurricane season, and there is always plenty of warning then if anything is brewing. Again, the *Yachtsman's Guide* is a must for cruising here. Bareboating has become so popular that despite the great number of boats, the most popular times, such as Christmas, Easter, and February and March, are usually booked up months in advance. There is a growing practice for charterers to rebook for the same period the following year as they turn the boat in at the end of a cruise in one of the peak periods.

As for the best harbors, there are so many that picking a few out seems ridiculous, but the Gorda Sound area is always a favorite, and

*The Baths, Virgin Gorda, a popular lunch stop.*

*Virgin Islands seascape.*

everyone has to make a lunch stop at the Baths on Virgin Gorda at least
once in a cruise. Of the places to eat ashore, we have always had the
best time at the zanily informal Last Resort in Trellis Bay. Those who
want to get a different atmosphere can branch out a bit by venturing
west into Vieques Sound between Puerto Rico and St. Thomas, where
the little island of Culebra has one of the best harbors in the whole area
in Ensenada Honda, which has several different anchorages within it.

# The Lesser Antilles

| | |
|---|---|
| AREA: | 12° to 17° N     61° to 62° W |
| | 300 by 60 miles |
| SEASON: | Year round, autumn not as desirable |
| PREVAILING BREEZE: | Northeast to southeast |
| CLIMATE: | Tropical |
| DRAFT LIMITS: | Not a factor |
| TIDAL RANGE: | 2 feet |
| NUMBER OF ANCHORAGES: | Unlimited |
| DRAWBACKS: | Occasional hurricanes, some racial trouble spots |
| PLUS FACTORS: | Climate, good breezes, choice of harbors, fishing, diving, swimming, easy navigation, sightseeing |
| BOOKS: | *Cruising Guide to the Windwards and Leewards; Street's Cruising Guide to the Eastern Caribbean* (vol. II and III); *A Cruising Guide to the Caribbean and Bahamas* |

Anegada Passage to the east of the Virgins, eighty miles of open, current-swept waters where the forces of the Atlantic and the Caribbean meet, marks the beginning, on its far side, of the Lesser Antilles, which stretch from here for over four hundred miles to within ninety miles of the South American mainland. The same general conditions as in the Virgins prevail here, but there is more open-water sailing as the trade winds blow in unimpeded freshness in the passages separating the islands, most of which are about thirty miles across. These can be wet and bouncy, although the boat is usually on a reach.

From a chartering viewpoint, the centers are Antigua and the

*The south coast of Grenada.*

*Curtain Bluff anchorage, Antigua.*

Grenadines, with some activity in Guadeloupe, Martinique, and St. Lucia as well. The islands between Anegada Passage and Antigua are not as frequently visited by yachts, as good harbors are scarce and there is no organized chartering based in this area.

Antigua's English Harbour is one of the major centers in the Caribbean, with many charter yachts, service facilities, and the picturesque surroundings of the restored Dockyard, where the British fleet used to base in Nelson's day. Antigua itself has quite a few good harbors and is worth a week's cruise at least, while from there south to the Grenadines, the big, mountainous islands only have one or two harbors on their leeward sides, and these are usually busy commercial centers.

The best sailing, in fact some of the best sailboat cruising anywhere, as I have already mentioned, is in the Grenadines, a sixty-mile-long chain of relatively low islands at the southern end of the Antilles, stretching from St. Vincent to Grenada, the last island south before

249

*English Harbour, Antigua, with Falmouth Harbour beyond.*

Venezuela. Here, as in the Virgins, there are many harbors close together, although there are some stretches that are exposed to the open Atlantic. In six cruises in the Grenadines, we have had some of the finest sailing of a lifetime. It is usually a reach, except for the passage north from Grenada, which goes by the notorious rock called Kick 'em Jenny that I have mentioned, and the average cruising boat can take a beating here. On one thrash past it, Jane and I arrived at Tyrrell Bay, Carriacou, in late afternoon, wet and exhausted, with a feeling of having played a tough game of football, and we fell into the sack before supper, saying, "If every cruising day were like that, we wouldn't cruise."

Since the bareboat charters all operate from St. Vincent, there is no need for visitors to go through this experience, but the five-mile reach across Bequia Channel at the start of a cruise from St. Vincent can be a good enough introduction to interisland passages. Fortunately, it is a short one.

*St. George's, Grenada.*

In the Grenadines, the passages between harbors can all be short, and there are some delightful stops, with the Tobago Cays as the absolute must for anyone in this area. They tend to be very crowded at the height of the season, but there is plenty of room, and the beachcombing and snorkeling are the best. The surroundings are un-spoiled and promise to stay that way, as the Tobagos are a national park and cannot be built on. Since there is no water there and they are too low to catch much rain, the problem is solved anyway.

There are several resorts for eating ashore in the Grenadines, such as Petit St. Vincent and Palm Island, and a few villages where the native life has not changed too much over the years. As I have said, if I had to pick between the Exumas and the Grenadines for one more cruise, it would be a tough choice.

# The Western Caribbean: Belize, Guatemala, and the Bay Islands

| | |
|---|---|
| AREA: | 15° 40' to 16° 40' N     86° to 88° 30' W |
| | 60 by 300 miles |
| SEASON: | Year round, autumn not as desirable |
| PREVAILING BREEZE: | East |
| CLIMATE: | Tropical |
| DRAFT LIMITS: | Not a factor |
| TIDAL RANGE: | 1 1/2 feet |
| NUMBER OF ANCHORAGES: | Unlimited |
| DRAWBACKS: | Occasional hurricanes, winter northers, heat, insects |
| PLUS FACTORS: | Unspoiled area, climate, good breezes, choice of harbors, fishing, swimming, diving |
| BOOKS: | *Cruising Guide to the Bay Islands of Honduras; A Cruising Guide to the Caribbean and Bahamas* |

An area that was only available to cruising yachtsmen with the time and inclination to make the long passage there in their own boats became accessible to charterers starting in 1978 when CSY established a bareboat operation at Roatan in the Bay Islands of Honduras. The western Caribbean had been an almost forgotten region for yachts until then, with very few boats passing through, and there are still vast areas that can only be reached by the adventurous leisure class. The big reef off Belize, where bareboating started in 1980, the waterways of Guatemala, and the Yucatan Peninsula remain almost untouched, with occasional visiting yachts, except for fishing fleets in Mexican ports.

The Bay Islands, going into the 1980s, were very much as they

*The south coast of Roatan.*

*The west coast of Baja California, Mexico.* (See p. 257)

have been for the more than one hundred years since they were ceded by England to Honduras and almost completely ignored by the outside world. The natives, largely of Anglo-Saxon stock and English-speaking, lived quiet lives as fishermen, seamen, shrimpers, and farmers, and their little world of islands, a perfect set-up for pleasant cruising, was relatively unknown.

Roatan is the major Bay Island, thirty miles long, fringed with a reef on its north coast and lined by a succession of good harbors very close together on the south coast. Off-lying to the east is Guanaja, and the Utila Cays are to the west, both with many anchorages and small cays set behind reefs in protected lagoons. Then, twenty miles to the south of Roatan, a fast reach across the trades, the Cochinos Cays are a miniature South Pacific world off by themselves, with one good harbor and a ring of smaller cays around a sparsely populated main island. This was our favorite area in a cruise there, although all the harbors on Roatan are good, and we particularly liked Port Royal, a wide harbor reached by two narrow cuts in a reef that is a paradise for

*Anthony's Cay, Roatan, Bay Islands.*

divers, as wrecks of pirate ships can be found there from the days when Henry Morgan made it one of his major bases. It was an out-of-the-way part of the world then, perfect for a pirate's hideout, and it still retains that feeling.

As usual, there have to be some cautions about an area. Winter northers from the great plains of North America reach down here several times a winter, bringing strong winds, rain, and low temperatures, and it is important to be in a harbor on the south coast of Roatan when a norther comes, as they all have fine protection.

In an April cruise there, we had the unusual experience of having the trade wind, normally a reliable 16–18 knots from the east, die out completely for four days. We were told, of course, that this never happens, and I'm sure it's rare, but when it did, the temperatures soared into the nineties and the sand flies came out to play.

We wouldn't let something like this keep us away from cruising here, and at the moment it offers about the last unspoiled cruising grounds in this hemisphere.

*A small boat harbor in Denmark's Fyn Archipelago.*

# In Foreign Waters

As the opening up of the Bay Islands to chartering shows, cruising sailors are always looking for new worlds to conquer, and there are many foreign areas where it is now possible to fly in and charter either a bareboat or a professionally crewed yacht. Here is a capsuled rundown of the ones I am personally familiar with, as a general guide on what to expect.

Somehow, as I have already admitted, I have missed two good cruising grounds fairly close to American shores, but reports from friends who have been there are generally enthusiastic. They are the widely contrasting areas of the Bras d'Or Lakes on Nova Scotia's Cape Breton Island, and the Baja California region of Mexico. The Bras d'Or have a short season of the three months of full summer, or perhaps even less cutting out September, although they are warmer and sunnier than the coastal waters of Nova Scotia, and less bothered by fog. It is a long slog to get a boat there on her own bottom, but chartering is now available. The atmosphere is one of rural peace and quiet, with many secluded anchorages.

Baja is only for the private owner, as Mexico has no chartering operations, and again it is a long slog there and back. Winter is the time to go, as the summers are hot, plagued by squalls and the possibility of hurricanes. It's a big area, with a tremendous choice of harbors and a good chance to see the life of isolated Mexican villages, along with the amenities of some fairly fancy resorts and a few sizable cities, such as Cabo San Lucas and Mazatlan.

North of Puget Sound, the inside passage to Alaska is not recommended as sailboat country because of extremely strong tidal currents, narrow channels, and uncertain and capricious winds. This is for the experienced powerboat skipper.

*Smögen, on the west coast of Sweden.*

In Europe, I have cruised in the Aegean, along the Dalmatian Coast of Yugoslavia, off Sardinia and Corsica, in Denmark's Fyn Archipelago, and through the skerries of the west coast of Sweden. These are all summer cruising areas, as Europe shuts up for sailors in the winter, even in the warmer parts of the Mediterranean. The Scandinavian areas naturally have the shortest season, really just July and August, when it is almost never dark. In the Med a couple of months can be added on each end, especially in the Aegean where it is actually better to cruise in spring and fall than in midsummer. Summer is very hot, and much of the Aegean is also subjected then to the strong "trade wind" from the north, called a meltemi, which can blast through at 40 or 50 knots out of a perfectly clear sky and blow for days on end. Sometimes it abates for a while, and it is usually lighter at night and in the very early morning. Those who do cruise in the summer make

*The usual afternoon lineup at Smögen.*

*Marina development at Porto Cervo, Sardinia.*

a practice of being underway either at night or in just the early morning hours. We have had delightful weather in the Aegean in May and October, and had some experience with the meltemi during a July cruise.

In Scandinavia, it seems as though the whole population is out cruising. Entire countries take a month off, as Sweden does in July, so this isn't far from the truth. Harbors are very crowded, but everyone is cheerful about shoehorning another boat in, and there is great camaraderie. Almost every boat has young children aboard, as family cruising is very big. No one ever seems to anchor out, as most of the harbors are man-made and anchoring would be in open waters. I particularly liked Tröensoe, Marstal, and Rudkobing in the Danish cruising, where

*An offshore island on the Dalmatian Coast of Yugoslavia.*

the atmosphere is quietly rural, with wheat fields and forests lining the shores, and picturesque little towns right out of Hans Christian Andersen ideal for exploring and for eating ashore.

In Sweden, Smögen and Fjallbäcka were among the more memorable of the quaint towns we poked into, and I have never seen such a concentration of cruising sailboats in one harbor as there was in the island port of Smögen, a quiet fishing village for most of the year.

Everyone is very weather conscious in Scandinavia, always worrying about it, and snatching desperately at whatever periods of sunshine there are. Bad weather can be a problem, but both my cruises (early August for each one) were blessed with idyllic weather.

In the Med, we cruised from Sardinia across the Straits of Boni-

*A few of the glossy yachts basing in Monaco.*

facio to Corsica and back in early June. The season had been on for almost a month, although it was still nicely cool. On an earlier visit, we had found late July weather ideal, and not too hot. The Adriatic in July provided very little wind for the Dalmatian Coast cruise, although the heat was not bad. One characteristic of the Med at all times of the year is a feast-or-famine situation with the wind, where it very often goes from flat calm to too much wind and back again without moderation in between. The resort towns of Yugoslavia were as full of visitors as any place I have been at that midsummer period, and the waters were crowded with visiting boats.

In all these areas but Yugoslavia, bareboat and professionally

262

*Entrance to the harbor of Monaco.*

crewed charter boats are available, although there isn't much of the latter in Scandinavia.

On the other side of the world, chartering is moving into the far reaches of the Pacific. An American-operated bareboat fleet of CSY 44s is now based in the Kingdom of Tonga in the central Pacific, and Australia, where sailboats practically grow on trees in the popular harbors, is waking up to the possibilities of bareboat chartering for visitors as well as home-grown sailors. Sydney Harbour, one of the great ones in the world from a yachting point of view, has bareboats available, and there are enough coves and bays in this mammoth complex to keep a cruise going for at least a week, with all sorts of sightseeing and shore-

*Patmos, Greece, in the Aegean.*

side eating as added attractions. The boats operate year round, as Sydney claims over three hundred twenty days of sun a year, and winter (July and August) temperatures are generally never below the fifties at the coldest.

The prime Aussie area, however, is the Whitsunday Island group in northern Queensland inside the Great Barrier Reef. This too is almost a year-round operation, although they do shut down in the midsummer months of January and February because of heat, high humidity, and the possibility of hurricanes. We had an eight-day cruise there in mid-September and have seldom experienced more delightful weather, more like a bracing summer day in the north woods of Maine

*The harbor at Patmos.*

or Georgian Bay than the expected tropical atmosphere at 20° latitude (south, of course).

We had two different boats, both modern fiberglass sloops comfortable for two at 29 and 33 feet and capable of taking up to six, and the islands reminded us very much of the Virgins in the way they were spread closely over about fifty miles. They are largely uninhabited except for five Out Island-type resorts, as the area is a national park, and there are interesting harbors galore, with great diving opportunities —we didn't see any sharks—and good reef walking and oystering around the harbors' edges.

The Barrier Reef, forty miles away to the east, makes a giant

265

*Paleokastritsa, Corfu.*

lagoon out of the waters inside it, so sea conditions are pleasant in the Whitsundays. Charter boats are not allowed out to the reef, as the navigation is tricky, but there is a service in which a small seaplane will pick you up off your boat at anchor and fly you to a lagoon in the reef for some low-tide exploration. In the islands the tidal range is as much as 16 feet, and tides must be carefully reckoned with at all times, and on the reef the rise and fall is about 6 feet. At low tide the coral just sticks out of the water, and it was an eerie experience to walk around it examining the fascinating reef life in its myriad hues and forms, completely out of sight of land on an empty seascape.

This was the highlight of a cruising area that is sure to attract more visitors, and an example of the way the whole world is opening up to the sailor who likes to cruise.

266

*Mykonos, Greece, in a meltemi.*

*Shute Harbour, Whitsunday Islands, Australia.*

# Bibliography

The Books listed here are referred to in Part III, "Where to Cruise," sometimes in more than one area. Some of them are out of print and only available through libraries or dealers in out-of-print books, and these are indicated. Prices are not given as these are subject to change, especially in the annually issued guides.

*A Cruising Guide to the Caribbean and Bahamas,* by William T. Stone and Jerry Hart (New York: Dodd, Mead & Co.).

*A Cruising Guide to the Chesapeake,* by William T. Stone (New York: Dodd, Mead & Co.).

*A Cruising Guide to the New England Coast,* by Roger Duncan and John Ware (New York: Dodd, Mead & Co.).

*A Cruising Guide to the Bay Islands of Honduras,* by Julius Wilensky (published by Westcott Cove Publishing Co., Box 130, Stamford CT 06904).

*Cape Cod: Where to Go, What to Do, and How to Do It,* by Julius Wilensky (published by Westcott Cove Publishing Co., Box 130, Stamford, CT 06904).

*Cruising Guide to The Florida Key,* by Capt. Frank Papy (published by Publication Arts Inc., 5700 Green Circle Drive, Minnetonka, MN 55343).

*Cruising Guide to the Windards and Leewards,* by Julius Wilensky (published by Westcott Cove Publishing Co. Box 120, Stamford, CT 0694).

*Cruises Mainly in the Bay of the Chesapeake,* by Robert Barrie and George Barrie, Jr. (Bryn Manwr, Penna: The Franklin Press—reissue of old book).

*Cruising the Pacific Coast,* by Carolyn and Jack West (New York: W. W. Norton & Co.).

Islands to Windaward, by Carleton Mitchell (Princeton, N.J.: D. Van Nostrand Co.—out-of-print).

*Ranging the Maine Coast,* by Alfred F. Loomis (New York: W.W. Norton & Co.—out-of-print).

*Sea Boating Almanac,* annual regional editions (published by *Sea* Magazine, 1499 Monrovia Avenue, Newport Beach, Cal 92663).

# Bibliography

*Street's Cruising Guide to the Eastern Caribbean,* by Donald M. Street, Jr.: vol. II, *Puerto Rico to Dominica*; vol. III, *Martinique to Trinidad* (New York: W.W. Norton & Co.)

*The Boy, Me and the Cat,* by Henry M. Plummer (published by the Catboat Association, P.O. Box 237, Mystic, CT 06372—(reissue of old book).

*The Bahamas,* by Linton Rigg and Harry Kline (New York: Charles Scribner's Sons).

*The Inside Passage,* by Anthony Bailey (New York: Macmillan—out-of-print).

*Waterway Guide,* annual regionl editions (published by Marine Annuals Inc., 238 West Street, Box 1486, Annapolis, MD 21404).

*Westward from the Virgins,* by Raymond N. Auger (published by Columbine Books, Box 2841, Aspen, CO 81611).

*Where to go, What to Do, and How to Do It on Long Island Sound,* by Julius Wilensky (published by Wescott Cove Publishing Co., Box 130, Stamford, CT 06904).

*Yachtsman's Guide to the Bahamas,* annual (published by Tropic Isle Publishers, Box 611141, North Miami, FL 33161).

*Yachtsman's Guide to the Greater Antilles—Virgin Islands, Haiti, Dominican Republic, Puerto Rico,* annual (published by Tropic Isle Publishers, Box 611141, North Miami, FL 33161).